# Capital Fundraising in the UK
## – the Compton Way

**Published in 2005 by Compton International Group Ltd**

Copyright © Compton International Group Ltd 2005

The moral right of Andrew Day and Paul Molloy to be identified as the joint authors of this work has been asserted in accordance with the Copyright, Designs and Patents Act 1988.

This publication may be reproduced free of charge in any format or medium for research, private study or for internal circulation within an organisation. This is subject to it being reproduced accurately and not used in a misleading context. The material must be acknowledged as Compton International Group Ltd copyright with the title and source of the publication specified.

For any other use of this material please write to:

Compton International Group Ltd
Compton House
High Street
Harbury
Warwickshire
CV33 9HW

First published in Great Britain in 2005 by Compton International Group Ltd
Compton House, High Street, Harbury, Warwickshire, CV33 9HW.

Tel: +44 (0) 1926 614 555
Fax: +44 (0) 1926 614 599

**www.ComptonInternational.co.uk**

British Library Cataloguing in Publication Data.
A CIP catalogue record for this book is available from the British Library.

ISBN-10: 0-9547519-0-6
ISBN-13: 978-0-9547519-0-6

Designed and typeset by Ark Creative (UK) Ltd.
Print production managed by John Moore, Norfolk.

# Capital Fundraising in the UK

## – the Compton Way

Andrew Day and Paul Molloy

# Contents

# Foreword

The UK's charitable sector has undergone dramatic changes over
the last 20 years. The 'Third Sector' is now made up of
approaching 190,000 not-for-profit organisations and has become
an industry with an annual income of over £32 billion. The UK has
the wealth to fuel this great charitable machinery – an estimated
£5.4 trillion in assets at the last count. It also has the human
resources to keep the cogs of the Third Sector turning. There are
now over one million trustees of charities and countless volunteer
workers. Yet, our people-packed islands still have major
infrastructural, social and community needs. There is hardly a day
when the financial demands of our education and health-care
systems alone fail to make front-page news.

Government cannot and will not be able to pay for it all – or
cost-effectively deliver all of the services needed by the UK's
citizens. Increasingly, our not-for-profit organisations are being
contracted to provide more – and asked to raise even more money
from their loyal donors and supporters.

As it stands, the sector's trustees, senior management teams and
fundraisers are not up to the fundraising challenges ahead.

Volume-based, quantitative, annual fundraising is in relatively
good shape in the UK. The knack of extracting small, regular
donations from many in 'appeals' is quite well tuned. However, we
have a serious skills shortage in successfully planning and
managing major gifts fundraising campaigns for capital and
endowment projects.

The UK's fundraising industry is largely geared to the percentage
games of direct response programmes, corporate partnerships,
grantsmanship and every conceivable kind of events fundraising.

Yet, in all of this activity, analysis and number crunching, a stunning and vital statistic has been overlooked: the wealthiest 1% of the UK's population possess almost one quarter (23%) of the wealth and, if taken further, the wealthiest 10% own over half (56%) of the wealth.

If the UK's charities are to play their proportionate role in the well being and quality of life of its citizens, we are going to have to learn how to be consistently successful in volunteer-led, person-to-person approaches to target big gifts and legacies.

This will not merely be a matter of recruiting North American fundraisers to replicate, 'Give, get or get off!' campaigns from their homeland. We have much to learn from the Americans, particularly the early godparents of the fundraising industry – but fundraising principles and methods need to be adapted to our traditions, our culture and our language. Also we desperately need to train and mentor our own major gift fundraisers.

We also need to remember what we have, sadly, forgotten. We have eminent institutions throughout the UK that were established and financially endowed centuries before our American cousins won their independence. Our major cities are packed with landmarks borne of the philanthropy and vision of the Victorians (who knew how reciprocal networks operated long before the development of systematic fundraising campaigns in the USA of the 1920s).

This book outlines how to plan and manage a capital fundraising campaign in the UK.

It originates from the authors' combined 40-year experience of managing volunteer-led campaigns. It is written with humility and gratitude to those who have gone before us: volunteer fundraising leaders and fundraising professionals with whom we have had the privilege to work and from whom we have learned, and continue to learn.

However, our book is also borne of frustration: that charities in the UK continue to waste so much money by not adapting and adopting tried and tested major gift fundraising principles and methodology.

Much of what you will find in the following chapters is organised common sense.

Common sense can take you a long way. Common sense and hard work can take you even further. Common sense, hard work and the support of volunteer leaders who are prepared to give their own money and approach others to do the same can make what appears to be impossible a reality.

**Andrew Day CFRE**
**Paul Molloy CFRE**
Compton International

# Acknowledgements

We would like to acknowledge all of the volunteer leaders who have given their money and their time on the campaigns we have personally planned and managed.

Without them, and the genuine partnership between volunteer and professional, fundraising goals would not have been reached and hospitals, universities, schools, cathedrals, hospices, theatres, community centres and a wide range of other institutions would be the poorer in both funding and social capital.

We would like to thank our colleagues, friends and families for putting up with the demands of the lifestyle that accompanies fundraising consultancy.

We would also like to thank our mentors – the people from whom we have learned and continue to learn.

# Table of figures

**Chapter 10**

# Chapter 1

# Capital fundraising in the UK: the Compton Way

## The 'accidental' fundraiser

The professional fundraiser, until very recently, used to be a rarity in the UK. Today, there are many thousands of fundraising professionals in our charitable sector. However, most of them, even if they are now fêted as gurus, will quietly confess to having found themselves in fundraising by accident rather than by design.

Perhaps they were at a loose end and a convenient, short-term job with a charity paid the bills. Perhaps they became disillusioned with graduate training in a big corporation and, in seeking a smaller business in which they could have greater responsibility sooner, found themselves working for a charity. Perhaps they passionately believed in a cause and wanted to make a difference. Perhaps, if more mature in years, with the experience of a first career behind them, they saw opportunities to share lessons learned in the commercial world with a growing not-for-profit sector.

Whatever the reason, even in the mid-1980s (when the co-authors of this book found themselves on an accidental career path) there were very few places in the UK where a young professional fundraiser could go to learn how to fundraise.

Trial and error was the norm, with the UK's accidental fundraisers learning by experience, ploughing through American 'how to do it' fundraising manuals and, in some cases, working for or with USA-based and other international consultancies to serve more practical apprenticeships.

What a difference 20 years can make.

## The UK not-for-profit sector today: a '£32 billion industry'

The Charity Commission's 2003–04 Annual Report *Shaping the Future* outlines the remarkable growth of the charitable sector in the UK with the following statistics:

- there are over 188,000 charities
- over 165,000 of these are 'main' charities (rather than branch or subsidiary bodies)
- the total annual income of the 'main' charities is £32 billion
- the estimated value of the total assets of registered charities is over £75 billion
- around 7% of charities receive nearly 90% of the total annual income
- the largest 471 charities (just 0.29% of those on the register) attract over 45% of the total annual income
- there are over one million trustees of charities.

## The modernised 'Third Sector'

In a relatively short space of time the UK's 'Third Sector' has been modernised.

The efforts of the willing amateur have been overtaken by Government-sponsored giving campaigns, industry associations, think tanks, specialist industry groups, conferences, seminars, workshops, every conceivable kind of training course, high-powered fundraising databases, cause-related marketing, merchandising, corporate social responsibility programmes, rapidly growing 'development offices' and volumes of research into giving trends and projections.

## The UK's community and social infrastructure creaking at the seams

Yet still our ancient cathedrals, churches and monuments are crumbling. Our universities, with the exception of Oxford or Cambridge, have insignificant or no endowment funding and insufficient operational capital to absorb political demand for greater accessibility. The schools that educate our children need books, technology and new buildings. Our hospitals and health care networks devour the funding granted to them by tax rises and still run major deficits. Our medical researchers spend half of their time filling out grant applications. Our museums open their doors without charging entrance fees and are in curatorial crisis. Our theatres and arts providers are only one or two non-populist productions away from disaster. The majority of our public sports and recreational facilities do not inspire us to move from the comfort of our sofas. Many of our community centres and village halls have seen better days.

## And we are a 'first world' nation

All of this is on our doorstep – never mind the demands and funding needs of the developing world which, reasonably, we should also be expected to support with capital investment, taxpayer-funded aid and charitable funding.

## Do we have the technology?

On top of this, rapid advances in information technology and telecommunications are changing the way our Government, institutions, suppliers and charities deliver their services. Much of our infrastructure seems to be in the wrong place, badly configured for the needs of today's user and lacking the quality or calibre to meet demand.

## Don't forget the environment

We have, at last, also discovered that we simply cannot build and hope for the best. There is an environmental price to pay for not thinking about what, why, how, when and where. We have inherited an environmental deficit from past generations of poor, expedient or unscrupulous planning. Sustainability, or fixing the unsustainability of the past, does not come without additional, short-term pain for long-term gain. There is hardly a town or city in the UK without a multi-million pound regeneration plan, with a lottery-funded 'flagship' project centrepiece.

In short, the community and social infrastructure of these small islands is creaking at the seams because of years (or some would say decades) of inadequate forward planning and funding.

## Consumer expectations

At the same time our expectations as consumers, stakeholders, clients, rate payers and voters have never been greater. We are no longer content to be treated in pre-NHS medical facilities or patched-up, 'NHS-branded' 1960s hospitals. The damp Victorian quadrangles in which we played as children are not good enough for today's generation of youngsters (and were probably not up to the job when they were inflicted on us). Why shouldn't our community swimming pools be as inviting and clean as those we have seen in North America or on the continent? Why do we still have to put up with no showers and muddy changing rooms when we turn out for our children's football matches on cold November Sundays? We are, after all, in the 21st century. Why shouldn't we want and demand more of an economically successful 'First World' democracy?

## Who's going to pay for it?

Of course we should expect our social and community infrastructure and institutions to advance and meet the needs of today's and tomorrow's generations.

But, who's going to pay for it?

## The Welfare State

The *Beveridge Report* of 1942 offered hope of reconstruction and regeneration to a war-torn nation, and became the blueprint for most of the 1948 legislation that established the Welfare State.

The impact of the two world wars on the UK is still very deeply felt, and the rebuilding of our social and community infrastructure is probably a superhuman feat of determination in the face of exhaustion rather than an inspired vision.

Sadly, much of the building and reconstruction of the late 1940s, '50s, '60s and '70s still exists and is operationally way beyond its sensible 'use by' date. (For example, our firm was contracted to a national, specialist hospital in which a new endoscopy suite was sited next to an existing ward. Nothing unusual in that – apart from the fact that following the patient's operation in the £1 million state-of-the-art theatre, they had to be wheeled down an uncovered slope in all weathers to the 'refurbished' ward: a converted 1940s prefabricated hut.)

## The demographic time bomb: stealing from our grandchildren

The National Insurance contribution, established in 1948, was increased recently to help to pay for the next generation of hospitals. However, no government can simply keep on increasing taxes and expect to be re-elected – and we are an ageing nation. The decreasing numbers of taxpayers of the next 20–25 years cannot be expected to pay for the growing numbers of pensioners. (Average life expectancy in the UK is set to rise to the age of 82 by 2045–50.) The tax base that supported the concept and establishment of the UK Welfare State is eroding and think tanks can argue all they want about progressive models of taxation – Government cannot and will not be able to pay for it all. We are, arguably, beginning to steal from our grandchildren.

## Public/Private Partnerships

Then came the dawn of Public Private Partnerships (PPPs) and Private Finance Initiatives (PFIs). These complex deals to contract out financial risk and services to the private sector in return for big chunks of capital funding are still in their early days, and have been controversial from the outset. Some argue that PFIs can work for suitable projects. Others are passionately against them for political and philosophical reasons. However, PPPs and PFIs show how it is possible for Government to work with the private sector to deliver new schools, hospitals and other major infrastructural projects.

## 'Additionality'

In some cases, PFI funding is being augmented by philanthropic and community fundraising campaigns for many millions of pounds. This, potentially, is where further genuine partnership between statutory bodies, companies, grant-making trusts, individual benefactors, suppliers, institutional stakeholders and the grass roots community can really make a difference. Not just to provide funding for 'finishing touches' on major capital projects, but to also create the social capital that interweaves charitable organisations such as our schools, hospitals, churches, libraries and universities into the social fabric of the nation.

## The wealth of the nation

Can private sector funding and philanthropy ever make a material impact on the nation's social, health, welfare and community needs? Well, with an estimated £5.4 trillion in assets, there is no lack of money in the UK.

However, as the websites and information services of wealth management firms point out, the UK's wealth is dramatically and unevenly spread across its population, with:
- the wealthiest 1% owning almost a quarter of the wealth (23%)
- the wealthiest 10% owning more than half of the wealth (56%)
- the wealthiest 50% owning almost all of it (95%).

If property is excluded from these statistics (and consideration given only to land, savings and shares) the uneven nature of wealth in the UK is even more pronounced, with:
- the wealthiest 1% owning a third of the wealth (33%)
- the wealthiest 10% owning almost three-quarters of the wealth (73%)
- the wealthiest 50% owning, near enough, the lot (97%).

## It has never been easier to be philanthropic

But, there is good news. Since the *Finance Act* 2000, it has never been easier or more beneficial to donors to give money away to a registered charity. Gone are the complexities of tax 'covenants'. A simple tick of a Gift Aid box will now suffice and gifts of quoted shares and other publicly traded financial assets have, at last, been able to draw income tax relief as well as the traditional capital gains tax relief. We do not yet have the progressive tax benefits of the USA, but Government has taken us in the right direction.

## Giving trends in the UK: growth over the last 25 years

In 2004, the Charities Aid Foundation (CAF) published the 25th anniversary edition of its annual *Charity Trends* report. This publication analyses the finances of the UK's top 500 charities in detail and offers the following insights:

- individual, charitable trust and corporate donors donated £4.6 billion to the UK's top 500 charities in 2003
- social care had the highest voluntary income (£1.08 billion), followed by health (£1.01 billion) and international causes (£875 million)
- the above levels of voluntary income were, respectively, equal to:
  - 8.6% of the Department of Health's (DoH) spending on social care
  - 2% of the DoH's spending on health
  - 25% of the Department for International Development's spending.

In other words, voluntary income is already of material significance – and is growing.

When CAF published its first trend report in 1978, the top charities had a fundraised income of £144 million. With an adjustment for inflation, this means that *the value of voluntary donations to charities from individuals, companies and charitable trusts has grown seven times over the last quarter of a century.*

Moreover, in spite of the Government-sponsored 'Giving Campaign' and regular features on the benefits of tax-efficient giving in the UK's quality press, CAF estimates that only one in three donors gives in a tax efficient way. An estimated £500 million in voluntary income could be added to current giving levels, if more donors were persuaded to make their giving tax effective.

## Are we any the wiser?

In short, we have packed 50 years of fundraising industry development into the last two decades, but have we really learned anything about successful, cost-effective fundraising? We can surely congratulate ourselves on being smarter – but are we any the wiser?

## Donor pyramids and all that

Most UK fundraisers are familiar with the concept of the donor pyramid (see Figure 1). This shows relationship building with prospective supporters from first acquisition gift through to major gifts and legacies. Over time, as a donor is worked up the pyramid, there are less givers but the gifts are bigger.

The trouble with the donor pyramid is that it still, seductively offers an infinite 'universe' of potential first-time givers at the base of the model. Unfortunately, this fits into the path of least resistance that 'all we need to do is get a million people to give us £1 each!'

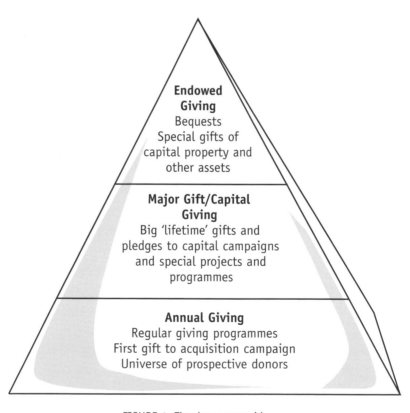

**Endowed Giving**
Bequests
Special gifts of capital property and other assets

**Major Gift/Capital Giving**
Big 'lifetime' gifts and pledges to capital campaigns and special projects and programmes

**Annual Giving**
Regular giving programmes
First gift to acquisition campaign
Universe of prospective donors

FIGURE 1: *The donor pyramid*

**FIG 1**

# A balanced fundraising plan: the three fundraising platforms

For many years now, Compton has used variations of the following 'Three Fundraising Platforms' model to better break down different kinds of funding needs, to highlight how best to respond to them in terms of methodology, programmes and promotional tools and to develop balanced fundraising plans:

| Annual funding<br>*Budget-driven*<br>*to sustain operations* | Capital funding<br>*Opportunity-driven to*<br>*fund special projects*<br>*and programmes* | Endowment funding<br>*Vision-driven*<br>*to secure the future* |
| --- | --- | --- |
| **Fundraising tools:** | **Fundraising tools:** | **Fundraising tools:** |
| Media appeals | Person-to-person approaches | Bequest programme to solicit legacies and other forms of 'planned gifts' |
| Public collections | Approaches for 'big gifts' | |
| Mail drops | Cash gifts, multi-year pledges, specific grants and gifts-in-kind | Person-to-person approaches |
| 'Mail and Dial' telephone campaigns | | Will-making campaigns |
| Gala events and dinners | Corporate partnerships Major donor recognition clubs | Legacy recognition clubs |
| Grass roots participation events and 'challenges' | | |
| Member-get-member programmes | Designated gifts and other naming opportunities | Targeted direct mail publications |
| Regular giving programmes | Exclusive information and cultivation events | Broad advertising and promotion |
| Merchandising | Grantsmanship | |
| Joint promotions and cause-related marketing | | |
| Recognition 'clubs' | | |
| Project and programme grantsmanship | | |

FIGURE 2: *The three fundraising platforms*

FIG 2

**Capital Fundraising in the UK: the Compton Way**    9

Essentially, there are three different kinds of fundraising need:

1. Annual/operational funding.
2. Capital funding.
3. Endowment funding.

Annual fundraising programmes tend to be volume-based and demand more people, institutional resources and operational budget than capital fundraising and legacy programmes.

## Fundraising costs

Fundraising should not be a hit-and-miss activity. It should be easy for charities to measure and monitor return on fundraising investment. However, cost can vary widely depending on the kind of fundraising and programmes not-for-profit fundraisers put in place. (For example, in a survey by CAF, fundraising costs for the 'Top 500' charities ranged from 1% to an incredible 51%.)

Certainly, if you are a trustee, finance director or director of development worried about the rising costs of fundraising, it would pay you to review high-cost/low-return fundraising methods and plan to roll out low-cost, high-return major gifts and legacy promotion activity.

## Fundraising fallacies

Sadly however, alot of UK fundraising still tends to focus on agency-driven letter-writing appeals; 'names on letterhead' patrons; glossy brochures; labour-intensive and time-consuming events, launches and merchandising. All engender false optimism that corporate social responsibility programmes will be an appropriate target, that grant-making trusts will give it all, or that an expensive, saturation PR or advertising push will convince everyone in the country to give a few pounds a month to 'this special cause'.

The above is, in the main, exhausting and low-return factory fundraising. The majority of trustees, board members, senior management teams and fundraising professionals know that it is exhausting and low return – and yet they still allow, and positively encourage, these things to happen.

## If you want money – you have to ask for it

If you want to raise money – you have to ask for it. The more directly and personally you ask for it – the more money you will raise. Furthermore, if you ask as one who has already given, your position is considerably strengthened.

## Capital fundraising: no 'plan B'

If your charitable organisation is one of the many in the UK facing a major, capital fundraising need (whether for bricks or mortar, programme-based work or endowment) it becomes even more crucial to adopt volunteer-led, person-to-person fundraising asking techniques.

Letter writing, house-to-house collections, events and other run-of-the-mill fundraising will simply not raise enough money.

## Capital fundraising 'campaigns': what are they, and where do they fit in?

Capital fundraising campaigns can be defined as the process of getting:
- as much money as possible
- as quickly as possible
- from, initially, as few prospects as possible
- using volunteer-led, peer-to-peer personal approaches
- for a specific project or programme.

Capital and endowment fundraising is the most cost-effective form of fundraising. For example, with full costs expressed as a percentage of the financial goals, the cost of campaigns planned and managed by Compton tend to fall within 3% and 8% of their targets.

## Excuses ... excuses?

So, why are person-to-person asking techniques for major gifts and legacy fundraising avoided like the plague in the UK?

Well, we don't like talking about money. We don't like the idea that we'll embarrass ourselves, or others (particularly our friends), by asking for money.

So, we hide behind the false hope that volume-based

fundraising techniques will raise the million (increasingly many millions) needed for our charitable projects. We claim that we already pay enough tax and that Government should pay for it. We state that it would not be in the ethos of our charity to use 'elitist', major gift fundraising techniques to target big gifts. We argue that such techniques were used elsewhere and failed. We claim that others, not us, should fund the need because we already do so much. We instruct our paid fundraisers to go and get the money. We complain bitterly and say 'I told you so!' when those fundraisers, generally, fail.

Still the wealthiest 10% of our nation has three-quarters of the money – still our ancient buildings crumble – still we stand ankle high in mud in the toilet-less changing rooms at Sunday football.

## What can we learn from the Americans?

American fundraising professionals from the 1920s developed systematic 'big gift' fundraising techniques. We can learn much from those early fundraising gurus, and their seminal texts and manuals are on all of our trainee consultants' reading lists. However, the mechanical delivery of quasi-evangelical fundraising dogma and jargon does not play well with the majority of UK charities and major donors.

## Can we be successful in major gifts capital fundraising?

Compton's experience tells us that it is possible to counter common objections about capital, major gifts fundraising and be successful in big gift fundraising in the UK. We need the right attitude (what our American friends and colleagues call 'mindset'). We then need to look at fundraising principles. Finally, the fundraising techniques have to be right.

## Successful capital fundraising: 'mindset'

If you believe that you are paying enough taxes already and that merely voting can preserve a democratic and civil society, then we probably don't want you on our fundraising team.

If you care, or are even slightly worried about the state of the world, believe that democratic freedom is fragile, believe that you have a responsibility to future generations and want to give something back to your community: step up.

## Successful capital fundraising: key indicators

We will not be asking you to run a fool's errand. Before a successful capital fundraising campaign is started, the following success indicators should be in place:

- **A positive image**
  Your charity must enjoy a positive image within its key internal and external audiences.

- **An urgent and attractive case for support**
  There must be a clearly demonstrable need and a strong consensus that the project is urgent and attractive.

- **A sensible plan**
  There must be a sensible plan to meet the need.

- **A sufficient source of contributable funds at the required levels**
  There must be adequate financial resources within the targeted audiences to meet the needs. As a guideline to the 'Scale of Giving' needed for capital fundraising campaigns the following patterns are helpful:
  - most multi-million pound campaigns achieve 80% of their target from only 100–150 gifts, of which:
  - the top 10 gifts usually account for 45%–55% of the target, which would include:
  - the largest gift at normally 10%–15% of the amount to be raised.

- **A supportive and enthusiastic governing body**
  Members of the governing body must be dedicated to the cause and willing to support it generously with money, time and energy.

- **Support of the wider, institutional family**
  The organisation must also enjoy the enthusiastic support of its staff and other members of its internal constituencies. The strong endorsement of those who are very closest to the organisation is an important indicator of the value and urgency of the fundraising campaign to the wider community.

- **Influential leadership**
  Your charity must have, or be able to forge, access to the kind of volunteer leadership, which can influence and motivate others. This, ideally, flows out of the governing body and is probably the most vital of all the essentials of capital fundraising.

- **A sense of urgency**
  A pervasive feeling must exist, or be developed, that the project is important and should be undertaken now.

## Successful capital fundraising: principles

With the fundraising essentials in place (and later chapters of this book will explain how to ensure that they are or can be put in place through the 'Resources Study'), it is time to see how best to put the following tried and tested principles into play for your particular organisation and campaign:

1. Leadership by example is the most important feature of a successful campaign. We cannot expect someone to do what we are not prepared to do ourselves. *Surely, common sense.*

2. Every member of the governing body, the voluntary campaign executive group and those closest to the organisation must give as generously as they can. These leadership gifts will be a major factor in raising the sights of other prospective givers to the project. *The tempered 'Give, get or get off!' message.*

3. People rarely give to causes. They give to people with causes. *One of the great fundraising rules.*

4. Prospective givers must be able to place their trust in the honesty and integrity of the institution involved. *Particularly in an age in which trust in institutions does not come easily.*

5. Prospective major givers should always be approached face-to-face. Only when asked clearly and directly, will they want to make a generous gift. *Would you give a charity the biggest donation of your life because it paid an agency to send you a letter?*

6. Prospective givers will be strongly influenced by someone they know and respect — and who has already given. *Peer-to-peer approaches are absolutely vital to maximise giving.*

7. People like to know what is expected of them. In asking for a gift, members of the fundraising team should clearly indicate the level of support being sought. *'What do you want from me?' is one of the most frequent questions in fundraising.*

8. Volunteer team members will usually obtain gifts of a similar size, or commitment, to their own. *Peer-to-peer benchmarking counts.*

9. People will often be persuaded to give more, when they are motivated by appropriate forms of recognition. *More of a factor than many will admit to.*

10. Prospective givers will be encouraged to raise their sights when given the opportunity to pledge contributions over a period of time. *There are very few prospective major donors who will simply write a cheque for £1 million.*

11. Publicity will help create the right climate for fundraising, but will not in itself raise a substantial amount of money. *We could tell you any number of stories of wasted time, money and effort.*

12. Fundraising campaigns that show early signs of success usually go on to achieve their targets. *It is all about building confidence and momentum. Money flows to money.*

These principles are at the core of successful major gifts fundraising and should be recognised as organised common sense.

## Successful capital fundraising: the volunteer giver and asker has the power

Finally, all of the previous steps will have been wasted without focus on the key asset of the capital, major gifts fundraising campaign: the volunteer giver and asker. The volunteer has the power in big gift fundraising. This can be a difficult message for the self-absorbed, multi-billion pound, professionally driven fundraising industry to accept. But it is true.

The leverage of a person of influence, wealth and power over a prospect in a peer-to-peer approach is absolutely at the core of successful capital fundraising.

Why this book?

The art and science of how to identify, cultivate, enlist, train and support volunteer major gift askers is desperately weak in the UK.

That is why we have written this book.

Drawing from the work of those in the profession who have gone before us; putting our own influence on it and, hopefully, passing it on to the next generations of capital fundraising professionals in the UK.

## Summary

- The UK has a £32 billion charitable 'Third Sector'.
- The UK's community and social infrastructure is over-stretched and needs large injections of capital and operational funding.
- Government cannot pay for it all.
- The UK is a wealthy country, but 10% of the population has 75% of the wealth.
- It has never been easier to be philanthropic but the UK's professional fundraising industry focuses on high cost, volume-based fundraising techniques.
- There are tremendous opportunities to plan and manage capital and endowment fundraising campaigns for tax-effective 'big gifts' in the UK.
- There are tried and tested fundraising principles and techniques that can be adapted to the UK culture and mindset to raise 'big gifts'.

# Chapter 2

# Donor motivation: why do people make major gifts?

## The psychology of big giving

Why do people make big gifts to charitable causes?

This question forms an inevitable part of the curriculum for most of the training courses available to today's inquisitive fundraisers – including our own, Compton campaign manager's course.

## What is a 'major gift'?

What constitutes a 'major', 'big' or 'top' gift depends on the nature of the organisation, the size of the fundraising goal and how the breakdown of that goal can be realistically achieved in a 'Scale of Giving'. But, as a rule of thumb, on most Compton-managed campaigns with goals over £5 million, giving levels in the £50,000 upwards range tend to be classified as 'major gifts'.

## Major giving: a two-stage process

First of all, it is important to recognise that most big giving is conducted in two stages.

Our experience, and that of previous generations of major gift fundraisers, is that the first stage of a big gift ask involves an 'emotional buy-in'.

With this in hand, the second stage of 'rationalising' the big gift (in the context of 'exactly how much', 'in what form' and 'over how long') comes into play.

Some giving motivations belong in the 'emotional' stage of the process; others relate more to the rational end of the spectrum, and inevitably, some crossover (see Figure 3 on page 32).

### The major reason for most major giving: someone asks

It needs to be acknowledged that, time and time again, there is one major reason why major donors make big gifts: because someone they know asks them to.

This is not just any old someone, but a peer: someone who is respected by the prospective giver and who can influence their decision-making – someone who knows the major gift prospect very well, and who is prepared to personally champion the charity's cause to that prospect.

### Don't get hung up on donor motivations

So, let's start at the beginning with pure major gift fundraising methodology.

If you as a fundraiser are doing your job well, you shouldn't have to worry too much about the psychology of donor motivation. You will have done your job by helping to recruit and train an appropriate volunteer champion to do the job for you – and he or she will know more about your major gift prospect and what motivates that prospect, than you will ever know.

Rather than getting too hung up on the theoretical scenario planning of donor psychology, time would be better spent working with your key volunteer to tailor and deliver the best possible approach for the major gift.

However, discussion about experience of donor motivations can help to shape and colour the big gift approaches that you plan and manage.

It is worth having the following list on hand as a backdrop. It is informed and compiled from years of experience of working with major prospects and givers in hundreds of fundraising studies and campaigns throughout the UK.

# Why major donors give: the 'Top 20' motivations

## 1. Because someone they know and respect asks them to give …

We cannot repeat this point enough for it to stay in the minds of those boards, senior management teams and professionals planning and managing major gift campaigns. There is absolutely no substitution for committed volunteer leadership making peer-to-peer approaches in capital/major gift fundraising. Volunteer leverage combined with visionary board members, inspiring executive team members and capable, supportive professional fundraisers is as close to a guarantee of success as you can get in major gifts work.

*'It's been a good fundraising campaign, and it's an excellent project. But I gave because the fundraising chairman asked me to.'* **(High six-figure giver to a school campaign.)**

## 2. Because they are expected to …

'Having no choice' hardly seems like an inspirational donor motivation, but it is increasingly the case in the UK as the 'leadership by example' message sinks in to governing bodies and other leaders of not-for-profits engaged in major gift work. This is not quite the same as the abrasive 'Give, get or get off!' message to board members and institutional leaders delivered by American fundraisers – but a less evangelical variation based on the realities of our analysis of hundreds of capital campaigns in the UK. Simply put, our experience suggests that those UK charities with governing bodies that take their fundraising responsibilities seriously will be more successful than those who continue to claim that they should have nothing to do with fundraising. Evidence alone proves that expectation needs to be in the motivation list. So, if you are one of the one million charitable trustees in the UK, you need to think about your role in giving and getting money for your cause. It is now, increasingly, expected of you.

*Governors*

*'You know what I'm going to ask. What is the board giving? Whether or not I take this application to the next stage will depend on this question being answered the*

*right way.'* **(Administrator of a major grant-making trust in a resources study.)**

### 3. Because they want to make a difference ...

If you are a trustee of a charity, one would hope that you are fully involved in the organisation and feel that you can make a difference. If this is the case, it should make your role in giving and getting money much easier. Of all of the common questions asked of our campaign managers by major gift prospects, the various forms of 'What difference will it make?' is the most frequent. You need to believe that your charity will make a difference and that you, and all of your fundraisers, are well equipped to explain how.

*'If they can really do what they say they are going to do – of course I'll give – and it will be generous. But I'll need to be convinced that the researchers believe that they can make a difference.'* **(High six-figure donor to a medical research campaign.)**

### 4. Because they want to give back ...

People who want to give back to a community, country, project or cause often make major gifts. They want to repay the good fortune or opportunity from which they have benefited. A classic example, from a dialogue that led to a massive gift to one of our major cathedrals:

*'He said that £11 million is a lot of money – and asked why he should make such a donation. I answered quickly by reminding him that he had made a fortune from the city and he should give some back.'* **(Adviser to major philanthropist.)**

### 5. Because of reciprocal social networks ...

An extension of peer-to-peer asking is peer-to-peer expectation – that what goes around comes around. If volunteer and major donor Smith asks peer and major gift prospect Jones, it is highly likely that Jones will be asking Smith for support for a favoured cause in due course. At High Net Worth (HNW) gatherings all over the world (and the UK is no different) latest news of generosity to charities is openly and freely shared.

'We also need to add X to our prospect list. Put him down for £500,000. I gave that to one of his charities a few weeks ago. Now it's his turn.' **(From a listing and prospect review session with a volunteer fundraising chairman.)**

## 6. Because they feel a sense of duty to give ...

In some, mainly established, wealthy families, there is a deep-rooted sense of noblesse oblige: a sense of duty to make charitable commitments to the community. Such giving is often found within the UK's big, charitable trusts and the concept of responsibility for giving is taken very seriously from one generation to another.

'Of course, X was the family's main philanthropist. He used to have great fun seeing the reaction of professors when he wrote them cheques for £1 million. He's gone now but the family have taken their responsibilities very seriously and have taken the time to consult widely on how best to continue giving money away.' **(Taken from a discussion with a volunteer fundraising leader about one of the UK's great, philanthropic families.)**

## 7. Because they are in the habit of giving ...

'We can't keep going to the same well' is one of the biggest fundraising fallacies we have to counter. The best source of future giving is from past donors. Fact. And being in the habit of giving – and enjoying it – is a big motivator of major givers. In our experience, the problems come when charities start to take their habitual donors for granted and forget to properly acknowledge their generosity.

'Yes, of course you should revisit the charity's old friends and donors. On a project of this size it would be unthinkable not to. The worst they can do is say no. But I very much doubt that this will be the case.' **(From a resources study interview with a benefactor who has made significant five- and six-figure gifts to the charity over the last 30 years.)**

## 8. Because of religious belief ...

The UK is a secular society compared to many and also today, of course, a multi-faith society. However, we still see our fair share of donors who give because of religious or faith-based motivation.

Some of the commitments we have witnessed over the years have been truly sacrificial (in evangelical Christian, Jewish and Islamic settings). However, whenever we see big, religious-inspired giving it tends to be directed to a faith-based project or a community in which that particular faith is practised. Generally (and we can say this authoritatively having worked in many different nations and with a wide range of faith groups) we believe that getting your relationship and dialogue right with the major gift prospect as a human being is more important than knowing a great deal about their religious or spiritual persuasion.

*'I am personally disappointed that so few people today choose to tithe and that the so-called 'Giving Campaign' talked only of persuading the wealthy to give away the equivalent of just 1% or 2% of their annual income. I expect to be asked for money, and I expect to allocate a portion of my annual giving for the next five years to this important project.'* **(Resources study interview – for a non-religious project.)**

## 9. Because of a moral, political or issues-based belief ...

While church going has decreased in the UK, it appears that involvement in a whole range of community and issues-based campaigns has dramatically increased. The UK has its fair share of both 'kitchen table' and large charities in this category, championing causes such as animal welfare, human rights, community lifestyle, protection of the countryside, international development and environmental causes. There is nothing like an urgent cause to raise big money. If you can solve the problem (if something can be built that will make a difference or something can be stopped that will preserve the status quo) there is usually big money within the reach of your cause.

*'The planning committee has not been truthful about the nature of the proposed warehouse site. The development, in fact, will offer tenant companies the right to bring in the heaviest kind of lorries and transport 24 hours a day. Up to this point, the action group has financed the campaign. We now need your financial support. We estimate that the next appeal will cost £10,000 and we need to know that this level of support is in place as because of the way the planning committee has acted,*

it needs to be lodged by the end of the week. Please call us on either of the following numbers within the next 24 hours to pledge your support. Thank you for helping us to preserve our quality of life in this special village.' **(Newsletter from a local campaign in a rural market town. Over £15,000 was raised in 24 hours. Two years on, the local action group has built up a £25,000 'war chest', a database of over 3,000 supporters and has forced the non-consultative planning committee to the negotiation table.)**

## 10. Because they seek self-advancement ...

Volunteers get involved in fundraising campaigns for all sorts of reasons. Some major givers – along with most of the nation's media – believe that the likelihood of knighthoods, peerages and other civil awards can be greatly enhanced by giving to the 'right' project or cause.

In North America, where self-advancement tends to be viewed as a less vulgar pastime, taking responsibility for leading particular fundraising campaigns can be regarded as a résumé-building essential. In the UK, participation in volunteer fundraising committees is increasingly being presented as a professional and social networking opportunity.

Being seen to 'do the right thing' as a newcomer to a new society, city or corporate market can be an important factor in major philanthropic and sponsorship giving. 'Aspirational' giving is the polite way to describe it. 'Buying respectability', 'social climbing' and 'influence peddling' tend to be used by those who don't want newcomers on their patch or who are, themselves, rather envious of the accolades being heaped on others.

While, occasionally, these kinds of major gifts are more transactional than philanthropic, most of the volunteer leaders we have worked with over the years who have been recognised for their charitable work have thoroughly deserved what they have been nominated for and received. And it is good to see that the UK is becoming more comfortable with the concept of self-advancement.

'London can be a tough place for a foreigner to break into social networks, even if they are creating massive shareholder value and being fêted in the financial press –

but I doubt that X would find your cause attractive enough to head up the fundraising campaign. We're after something a bit more establishment – and, as for awards, we've already got someone working on that.' **(International marketing director of a company speaking on behalf of a senior executive we targeted – and failed to get – to lead a major fundraising campaign.)**

## 11. Because they want recognition ...

Equally, the desire for recognition motivates more major givers in the UK than we would probably like to admit. Ten years ago, when we tested donor recognition concepts in fundraising resources' studies, we frequently met comments such as, 'No, I can't see a major benefactor wanting their name all over the new building. It would be far too American.' But, there has been a noticeable shift in attitude to naming rights and other forms of major gift recognition over the last decade.

Today, the majority of our clients have buildings, parts of buildings, programmes or special funds named after major donors (often with little thought about how much, for how long and how this impacts on future fundraising efforts). In the current climate of political correctness one would have thought that high-level donor recognition clubs (in which donors are given various titles depending on the level of their contribution) would be avoided. Our experience has been exactly the opposite.

And, of course, one of the most highly prized forms of recognition is for a big gift to be presented anonymously when the donor's identity is obvious to everyone. We seldom see examples of major donors trying to buy 'immortality'. Most prospects and donors we meet think more deeply than that. However, fundraisers in the UK often underestimate the value of recognition as a donor motivation and sight-raising tool.

'Of course the naming right made a difference. Before we offered to name the building after him there was only £3 million on the table. We ended up with £5 million. That's precisely £2 million worth of difference.' **(From a discussion with a vice chancellor about naming a new university building.)**

## 12. Because they want to commemorate others ...

At the other end of the recognition spectrum, we see commemorative giving: where major donors give to celebrate the life or work of another and have this recognised by a wider public. In memoriam giving is usually instrumental in medical research, hospital, hospice and other health care fundraising campaigns. We see six and seven figure naming rights taken up to commemorate family members and other loved ones.

In the religious setting we have seen big gifts made to name projects and 'dedicated gifts' within those projects after priests, nuns and other saintly or charismatic leaders. We have seen college and university buildings and programmes named after alumni and teaching staff. Many grass roots community fundraising campaigns – usually well supported by local media – tend to be focused around the personification of the charitable cause in the form of commemorative giving. Commemoration is a strong, unselfish and emotive reason for major giving.

*'How much do I need to give to name a room? I'd like it in the name of my wife's late father who died in the hospice last year.'* **(A donor who led by example on a hospice campaign with a five figure 'composite' gift involving the sale of an asset, gift of shares, cash pledge and a legacy.)**

## 13. Because of nostalgia ...

Major donors sometimes give because they have fond memories of a place or event in their shared history with a not-for-profit institution. Schools, colleges and universities in the UK are still, generally, not as sophisticated as their counterparts in North America at organising alumni reunions (and knowing where such gatherings and events fit into fundraising). But nostalgia is not just limited to alumni fundraising, as our hospital fundraising experience has taught us:

*'The hospital tour wasn't going well. He didn't seem to be impressed by anything we showed or told him. He didn't want lunch. The medical director was clearly finding him hard going. Then we walked him through the old children's ward and schoolroom. It was like dealing with another person. His eyes lit up. He smiled. He*

started to talk about his time at the hospital as a child.' **(One of our consultants reporting back on a visit from a 75-year-old benefactor prospect who had spent a number of years in and out of the hospital as a young child. A week after the visit he made a £1 million gift to the hospital's redevelopment campaign.)**

## 14. Because of civic pride ...

We have, over the years, worked on many hundreds of heritage and regeneration projects – historic buildings, great cathedrals, theatres, arts centres, galleries, monuments and civic centres. The wish to live in a 'nice place', to make where one lives a 'better place' or to pass on to or conserve something for future generations is at the core of many fundraising campaigns.

For civic-based projects to work well, they need to be genuine partnerships between Government (whether it's local, increasingly regional powers or Westminster), the private sector and the grass roots community. Token participation from any of these important stakeholders leads to the 'white elephant' projects that, sadly, appear to have taken up so much time, money and media space over the last decade or so. Thankfully, for every Millennium Dome, there have been a thousand meaningful and less high profile projects involving hundreds and thousands of citizens keen to safeguard, improve or regenerate their communities. At the local government level we still have much to learn from other countries about how to plan, fund, manage and deliver capital projects. But, if properly thought through, resourced and implemented, there should never be a lack of volunteers for civic-based projects and programmes in the UK.

'Of course it's difficult. But it's been difficult here since we lost our manufacturing industry. This project is the flagship at the heart of the regeneration of this city. It's unthinkable that I wouldn't be involved and get others to join me in working through the issues to bring greater investment, prosperity and cohesion to our community.' **(Leading fundraising volunteer from a Midlands cultural/regeneration project.)**

### 15. Because of enlightened self-interest ...

It could be argued that self-interest lies at the heart of half a dozen of our major donor motivations, but some have more self-interest than others (for example most Corporate Social Responsibility (CSR) programmes and many major donations to political fundraising campaigns). This is not to say that major donations from CSR programmes or political parties are lacking value. Individual volunteers from major companies are central to many of the project teams we manage, and giving money to and working for your political party of choice is an important part of the democratic process. But CSR programmes would not exist if companies did not have a licence to operate in those communities and did not feel the need to prove their community credentials to shareholders, employees, politicians and local community groups.

'Don't try and negotiate with me. Be very clear about that. Negotiation will not help you. We support regeneration and community projects in the local community. We do that for very obvious reasons. We can see them from our boardroom. Our employees can get involved – and they like that. But, we do need something to show our female employees that we care about them. So let's see if we can find a way to do something together from that angle.' **(Interviewing a CSR director from a bank.)**

### 16. Because of tax benefits ...

The need for tax benefits is very seldom the prime mover for a major gift (which, in the first instance, tends to be driven by more emotive forces). However, illustrations of tax-effective charitable giving can be invaluable in raising the sights of a benefactor, but – usually – only once the emotional decision to make a major commitment has already been made.

'Are you sure about this? If these illustrations are right, I won't pay any income tax next year.' **(From discussions with a seven figure major donor to a hospital project. Our outline illustrations were accurate and the hospital benefited from a major gift of shares.)**

## 17. Because of spite ...

In the 12th century a brilliant Jewish scholar (Moses ben Maimon – or Maimonides) wrote powerful words about the importance of giving to charity and how best to do it. In the Maimonides Order of Giving, the lowest form of donation is to give begrudgingly, letting everyone know how much you have given and that it has been done in a reluctant manner. Fortunately, we see little of that, and high levels of inspirational giving. However, we do occasionally see what could be described as 'spiteful' or 'vengeful' giving motivations.

We have been present when individuals have threatened to cut individuals or charities out of their wills (benefiting others in the process), and we were once asked by a group of nurses if they could club together to name the 'bed pan room' after an unpopular ward sister. Is a spiteful act of giving cleansed by the innate charitable impact and benefits of a major gift? The subject of another book perhaps – and, to use a good British phrase, 'there's nowt so queer as folk.' However, have no doubt, if you or your organisation treat people well, they will usually find a way to say thank you. If you do not treat people well, you may sometimes get what you deserve.

'They made it clear that not only was I, in their opinion, not good enough for them – but that I would never be good enough for them.' **(A wealthy entrepreneur, currently in negotiation with a 'new university' in one of the UK's ancient university cities for a pledge/bequest of £10 million.)**

## 18. Because of guilt ...

We live in an uncertain world in which it appears possible to count one's blessings almost on a daily basis. Global disasters seem to get worse and more frequent, and in the culture that originated the Band Aid project, latest generations of pop stars encourage us to 'Thank God it's them, instead of you!' Whatever works to get the message across and the money flowing – and guilt does occasionally yield major gifts.

'I felt uncomfortable when I saw how so little money could change life so dramatically. There but for the grace of God. Yes, you could call it guilt. I'm relieved it's not my grandchildren in those pictures.' **(Major donor to an international medical charity.)**

### 19. Because of genuine altruism ...

Thankfully, the majority of major donors we deal with give because they recognise that someone they know and respect is asking them to support a powerful cause. And, for every donor who is triggered by a less pure motivation, we see ten who give because they feel an instinctive, human need to do so.

'Apart from the fact X has asked me — it's the right thing to do. I've been looking for something meaningful to do: a home for my giving and volunteer work. Now I've found it — at least for the next five years.' **(Major donor and volunteer on a hospital campaign.)**

### 20. Because of good karma: what goes around comes around ...

Sooner or later, anyone who spends time around HNW major philanthropists will pick up references to 'what goes around comes around'. There appears to be no logic or research backing up this motivation. It appears to be based on the experience of serial major donors who have lots of money and who give lots of money away. But it appears to be true. The more major donors give away — the more prosperous they seem to get. Is this just self-obsessed nonsense, or is there some divine reason for it all? Who knows, but it is real enough for a number of private client divisions of banks to be mentioning it in their HNW and ultra HNW client briefings.

'It's true. I can't tell you for sure when I first noticed it. I'd like to think it was after I'd made my first £1 million donation, but I can't be sure. But, I'm sure it's true. The more money I've given away — the more money I seem to make.' **(A very wealthy fundraising volunteer leader.)**

## Move past the theory and start asking

It is crucial to take a step back: to pause for thought before making a major gift approach, and it is useful, as part of this final, 'pre-ask' check, to review the backdrop of the prospective donor's possible motivations. If you have done your job well, the volunteer champion who is helping you to access and approach the prospect will know the make up of the prospect anyway: probably much better than you ever could. So, be careful not to over work the psychological scenarios as they can create doubt, variables and hesitation.

Fundraising is not an academic process, but mostly organised common sense.

In most situations, if you have the right volunteer asker approaching the right prospective giver, the greatest psychological challenge to a fundraising professional is to get that volunteer champion to move past the theory and to start asking.

**Emotional**

- sense of duty
- recognition
- nostalgia
- spite
- guilt
- altruism
- commemoration

- personal approach by a peer
- expectations of others
- want to make a difference
- want to give back
- civic pride
- good karma
- religious belief

**Rational**

- habit
- moral, political or issues-based belief
- self-advancement
- enlightened self-interest
- tax benefits

FIGURE 3: *Top 20 major donor motivations in the context of the emotional or rational spectrum*

**FIG 3**

## Summary

- Major giving is a two-stage process.
- Prospective major givers, first of all, 'buy in' emotionally.
- Then they rationalise how best to make the major gift.
- A 'checklist' of donor motivations is a useful tool to help prepare your volunteer askers.
- Don't get too hung up on the academic side of fundraising.
- Fundraising is mostly organised common sense.
- There is only one way to get big money.
- Ask for it.

# Chapter 3

# Beginning the campaign: the resources study

Change *always* brings challenges.

When your organisation changes, when it grows or decides to reorganise, you'll probably face significant financial challenges, such as the requirement to fund a new project or programme. In these circumstances the investment needed is usually best secured, at least in part, by mounting a capital fundraising campaign.

## Do we mount a campaign or an appeal?

Remember that we defined a capital fundraising campaign in Chapter 1 (see Figure 4). A capital fundraising campaign is not a broad-based community appeal for funds from the wider public (although a grass roots community appeal may come later).

**Capital fundraising campaigns:**

◎ **raise as much money as possible**

◎ **as quickly as possible**

◎ **from (initially) as few gifts as possible**

◎ **using volunteer-led, peer-to-peer personal approaches** ✗

◎ **for a specific project or programme.**

FIGURE 4: *Definition of a capital fundraising campaign*

**FIG 4**

## The first step to successful campaigning ...

To begin, you need to work out:

- where the money might be for your specific project
- who in particular is sufficiently inspired by what you propose to make a gift themselves and ask others to join them in doing so.

While it is accepted common sense to look before you leap, it is surprising how many don't bother to even try to answer these two questions and just jump straight into multi-million pound fundraising campaigns.

This heroic 'in at the deep end' mentality has led to some epic institutional 'sinkings' – all for the want of a bit of common sense in testing the water first to take some sensible soundings. While there is little as positive for the long-term well-being of an organisation than a successful capital campaign, sadly the consequences of failure can be devastating.

Clearly, when considering whether or not to make the considerable investment required to mount a capital fundraising campaign, the fiduciary responsibility to complete some form of due diligence is paramount. Otherwise your fundraising campaign runs the very real risk of starting out in an entirely unproductive direction.

By deciding to conduct a fundraising resources study, your campaign, if it proceeds, will do so on a sound footing with a clear target, plan and identified sources of both volunteer leadership and money.

## Guidance from your godparents

In a nutshell, a resources study is a qualitative research process that identifies your organisation's readiness to mount a capital campaign. In some respects, the resources study can be regarded as a visit to your institutional godparents to seek the benefits of their wisdom before you embark upon a major venture.

The combination of your godparents' *influence* and *affluence* (and their access to others with these qualities) is usually impressive. Their willingness to get involved in your project, at this important time in your institutional development, will be a crucial success factor for your campaign, if it proceeds.

## What form does the study take?

The resources study is based on a series of confidential interviews with a cross-section of your organisation's leaders, givers, influential friends, staff members and other prospective supporters.

The response of these key constituencies to your proposed project, and their guidance on how best to make it a financial and community relations' success, will determine if and how you make your campaign public.

Based on the information gathered, your study director's professional experience and other research data, the study report should recommend a clear way forward. It is worth remembering however, that not all resources studies lead smoothly on to the mounting of a campaign. On occasions the information gathered, when analysed in the hard light of day, causes us to recommend that the most sensible way forward would be for our client to take an alternative course of action.

## Study tools

To complete a resources study you need to develop three important tools:

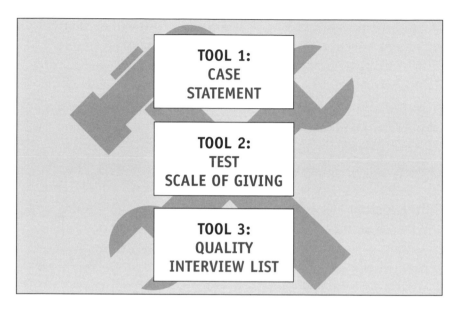

**TOOL 1:**
**CASE**
**STATEMENT**

**TOOL 2:**
**TEST**
**SCALE OF GIVING**

**TOOL 3:**
**QUALITY**
**INTERVIEW LIST**

FIGURE 5: *Resources study tools*

FIG 5

## Tool 1: Case statement

You have a clear understanding of what it is that you want to raise funds to achieve, but can you communicate your thinking to others? Start by drafting what is known as a 'case statement' – a concise two-page document that:

- tells all that needs to be told
- answers all the important questions
- reviews the arguments for support
- explains the proposed plan for raising the money
- shows how gifts may be made
- presents the people who vouch for the project and will give it leadership and direction.

### Really work through the thinking

Ensure that your fundraising committee and fellow board members actually share the ideas put forward in your concise case statement.

Take the time to get the views of these key stakeholders

incorporated into the document. We're not saying that the committee should do the drafting, because frankly there is nothing more painstaking than this, but rather, that the arguments for raising the money are well 'thrashed out' by your leadership team.

In our experience when the aspirations for your organisation are first presented in black and white, there is *always* further work to do to ensure that the case faithfully presents the aspirations for the future. But do please keep the case brief and free of jargon, or it simply won't be read. Remember too, that at this stage of the process there's no need to make a meal of the case statement – it should look and feel like an advanced draft document, not a finished piece.

### Telling a story

Start by sketching out your answers to the following questions, as if you are telling a story to a trusted friend from whom you are seeking their thoughts and guidance:

1. **Your reason for being** – Why is your organisation in existence; what are you here to do today? Resist reverting to the 'management speak' of an often tired or over-worked mission statement; just say it as it is, in plain English.
2. **History** – Where has the organisation come from? Just a paragraph of background information to help set the scene for your story.
3. **Achievements** – What have been the high points? Explain where your organisation has enjoyed success.
4. **Challenges** – Outline what the future looks like and where the opportunities lie.
5. **Response** – Share your thoughts on how the project will respond to these challenges and help your organisation to fulfil its reason for being.
6. **Project benefits** – Describe how your project is going to change things and deliver clearly defined benefits. Remember that the key motivator for giving is not need, but *opportunity*.
7. **Cost breakdown** – Just give the overall project cost estimates in broad strokes. There's no need to have the quantity

surveyors working overtime, but if you're asking people to invest big money in your project, they will certainly want to know how the numbers stack up.

8. **Proposed fundraising methodology** – If you want to raise millions of pounds, make it clear in your case that you are proposing to do so using peer-to-peer personal asking, not public appeal methods with which most people will be familiar.

9. **Pace-setting leadership** – Indicate who the leaders are for the proposed campaign and what pace-setting gifts have already been committed to the project.

10. **Recognition** – Explain the thinking behind the types of recognition that you would like to offer potential givers to the campaign.

11. **Tax effectiveness** – Confirm that your organisation is a registered or exempted charity and therefore able to benefit from Gift Aid, payroll giving schemes, gifts of shares and so on.

12. **Your guidance and input is needed** – The first ask. Ask for help from those with whom you'll share the case statement; by clearly seeking their input you'll turn an interviewee into a prospect.

13. **Vision for future** – Sign-off with a 'Churchillian' reaffirmation of the benefits that your project will deliver.

Remember to be concise and use plain language when drafting your case statement. Include conceptual architect's drawings, artist's impressions and people-based photographs to also help interviewees to visualise the project, the community and personal benefits that will flow from it.

### Who are we writing to?

One of the most important rules when drafting any document is to remember who will be reading it. For the case statement, the first audience will be the people to be interviewed as part of the resources study.

Ahead of their appointment with the study director, interviewees should be sent a copy of the case statement, with a letter confirming the arrangements for the interview. In so doing, interviewees will be given the courtesy of time to review the case and reflect on not only what is proposed, but also where the money might come from. This simple step considerably improves the validity of the study findings.

Once the interviewees have had their say, the case statement can be amended and developed further, often becoming a larger document, known by professional fundraisers as a 'case for support'.

## Case for support

Large and complex capital campaigns need to have developed a comprehensive argument that supports the call for funds from all perspectives. The case for support is a more detailed version of the concise case statement – it details the background on:

- the expanded thinking behind the vision for your institution
- the detailed options that were considered about the project and its funding
- the arguments that can be presented to all the different stakeholders, to convince them to support the campaign
- an analysis of the external environment for the campaign, including details of competing calls for funding within the organisation and in the wider community
- the background of all the key campaign leaders and the specific roles they have agreed to play
- a comprehensive financial report on your organisation, reviewing attached annual accounts and building the argument for raising philanthropic funds.

The fact is, you can spend *years* writing a case for support, when usually all that is needed is a slightly extended case statement and a collection of key appendices, such as your annual accounts.

**One story to tell**

At the end of the resources study, having reviewed the comments made by the interviewees, you will have:

- one document from which you can draw the copy for your promotional material, grant proposals and written submissions to benefactors
- one document that you can amend and keep up-to-date as your campaign unfolds and funds are raised
- one story for all your team to tell.

In Chapter 11, when we discuss campaign publicity and public relations, the case statement is once again at the centre of the messaging for your project and the reasons for raising a large amount of money. So, taking the time to bring together the thoughts and arguments in one concise form to be tested and developed throughout your campaign provides an invaluable and indispensable fundraising tool.

Finally, if the story of your project cannot be written into a concise, positive case statement that justifies its objectives, you need proceed no further with your planning for a study. Without a well-considered and compelling case, your fundraising plans are best shelved.

## Tool 2: Test scale of giving

Most of us, when we consider a multi-million pound fundraising target, have great difficulty contemplating how it might be raised. We are personally not used to dealing with sums of money of this magnitude.

In order to help focus attention and effort on securing gifts of a sufficient size to achieve the goal, a scale of giving is first developed as a test document for use during the resource study interviews.

The test scale of giving is a table demonstrating a pattern of gifts that, if secured, would ensure a fundraising goal is achieved. The scale shows exactly how many gifts need to be secured, and at what levels, for a funding goal to be attainable.

Ahead of the study interviews, the study director would draw up a test scale of giving based on past experience of capital fundraising and previous levels of giving to that and other similar institutions.

## Experience counts ... how the numbers stack up

In our experience in managing over a thousand capital fundraising campaigns:

- most multi-million pound campaigns achieve 80% of their target from only 100–150 gifts, of which:
- the top 10 gifts usually account for 45%–55% of the target, which would include:
- the largest gift at normally 10%–15% of the amount to be raised.

The test scale of giving is reviewed with interviewees during the resources study and it is subsequently adjusted depending on their comments about where funds may be for your project, before the campaign gets underway.

| Size of annual gift £ | Size of gift over five years £ | Number of gifts required | Totals £ |
|---|---|---|---|
| 300,000 | 1,500,000 | 1 | 1,500,000 |
| 200,000 | 1,000,000 | 1 | 1,000,000 |
| 100,000 | 500,000 | 4 | 2,000,000 |
| 50,000 | 250,000 | 6 | 1,500,000 |
| 20,000 | 100,000 | 9 | 900,000 |
| 15,000 | 75,000 | 12 | 900,000 |
| 10,000 | 50,000 | 20 | 1,000,000 |
| 5,000 | 25,000 | 25 | 625,000 |
| 2,000 | 10,000 | 30 | 300,000 |
| 1,000 | 5,000 | 35 | 175,000 |
| 500 | 2,500 | 40 | 100,000 |
| | | 183 | £10,000,000 |

FIGURE 6: *Test scale of giving for £10 million over a five-year pledge period*

FIG 6

Ultimately, the scale of giving is the main tool used when asking a potential giver for money. Care must be taken during the study not to present a scale that will lower the sights of the prospective major givers, or unnecessarily exclude most of the constituency, simply because the lowest suggested giving level is set too high. When using a scale, we usually explain that gifts would be gratefully received above as well as below those indicated – and that the scale is designed to help focus the fundraising effort to ensure all those approached as part of the campaign understand the level of giving needed to ensure the target is achieved.

## Where's the money to be found?

During the study interview, it is only when the interviewee is considering the scale, that discussion turns to exactly where the money might be found for the campaign and who should ask for it. Some interviewees also use the example of the giving of the 'average' person, as a way of indicating the level of gift they would be prepared to make, if the campaign proceeded.

A skilful and experienced study director will be able to guide a study interviewee around the test scale of giving, in the process learning about what will motivate their level of giving, but also those who they know and may be prepared to approach. It is a pivotal moment for planning a campaign, particularly when the discussion is centred on the source of those top 10 gifts that could deliver half the target.

## Tool 3: Quality interview list

A resources study is only as good as the calibre of the interviewees. As we have said before, successful capital campaigns need to access influence and affluence.

Your organisation will probably be able to secure the help of such influential people (albeit, sometimes, two or three spheres removed from your core constituency). Start by approaching your organisation's godparents for an interview. Ask for their help to expand the interview list, to seek out the corners of your organisation's network, to speak to people who are probably just beyond the usual circle of current supporters.

### Quality not quantity

Remember too that the resources study is a qualitative research process. Most experienced fundraising consultants will quietly admit that positive studies hinge upon the comments of half a dozen powerful interviewees. This applies to campaigns big and small, so aim to interview between 25 and 35 carefully selected people.

When drawing up this list, consider the various constituencies within your organisation – board, staff, current givers, neighbours, suppliers and so on. Then think a little more creatively about who exactly would like to see this project happen. Who might gain some benefit, no matter how remotely, from what you have in mind. Then pool all these names into a master list, where it will become clear that some names just keep reappearing, some are well known and others will need some careful research.

Once you have consulted widely and drawn-up your master list of possible interviewees, then with 'fresh eyes' prioritise the list based on who you really believe can help you get the money. Do not be tempted to include the names of naysayers who you know are against the project or even those who might be included for simply representative reasons.

In the UK it is not usual practice to do as the North Americans do and conduct resources studies that involve interviewing 100 people or more, at vast expense. Frankly, if you spend the time carefully selecting the right people to interview, covering countless others usually brings forward the same information, adding nothing more to the investigation – except a nicely padded report. So, the secret is to take the time at the outset to ensure that you interview the *right* people, rather than everyone you can think of.

### Getting access to the 'great and good'

Now that the list is fine-tuned, work out who is best placed to make an initial contact with the proposed interviewee to ask if they would be prepared to give their guidance and advice to your organisation as it prepares for this major campaign. It is only through this personal, often informal contact that interviewees are approached and agree in principle to give their time to meet with the study director. Assurances usually need to be given that whatever comments the interviewee chooses to make will not be directly attributed to them in the report and that the interview is not some convoluted cover to ask them for money (at this time).

## Setting the scene ...

Once these three preparatory tools have been developed (Case, Scale, List), it is time to get on with the all-important personal interviews.

The shape and direction of study interviews will vary from project to project and interviewee to interviewee. Generally, we do not recommend the preparation of formulaic checklists or questionnaires completed by the study director, as this creates a tendency to push pull interviewees through their responses.

Conducting resources studies is as much of an art as it is a science: 'gut' instinct as much as empirical evidence. Inexperienced interviewers generally let the mechanics of the process get in the way of an intuitive reading of what the interviewee is really thinking and feeling about the project.

A good study director creates a professional but relaxed environment in which interviewees feel they can speak their minds.

## Asking the right questions ...

As a result of the resources study, your organisation should have honest answers to the following questions:

1. Is your organisation's community relations environment conducive to fundraising success?

2. Is the project regarded as attractive, urgent and worthy of financial support at high levels?

3. Is the test scale of giving realistic and attainable?

4. Is the volunteer leadership necessary for the success of the campaign available?

5. When should you embark upon your campaign – and over what period of time?

6. Are your board and management team ready and willing to successfully mount a capital fundraising campaign?

## Winning your fundraising campaign on paper

In getting frank answers to these key questions through a detailed resources study report and preliminary action plan, your organisation begins the important process of transferring ownership of the fundraising project to volunteer leaders and 'winning the campaign on paper'.

When the study interviews have been completed, remember to thank all those who gave their time to this process. Having identified them and provided information on the plans for the campaign on which you have sought their input – you're half way to the money. (See Chapter 4 for further explanation of the prospect cultivation process.)

## Improving your chances of success

A properly conducted resources study can on occasions lead to immediate leadership gifts to help get your campaign off to a solid start. These first givers are also often those who will be willing to lead your campaign, if the issues they raised in your study are properly addressed.

As we will discuss in greater detail in Chapter 4, the process of prospect development increases the probability of *getting gifts*, as well as improving the *size* of the gifts received. Your resources study is an excellent mechanism for beginning this process.

By taking the time to succinctly summarise the case for the campaign, then inviting those that you believe will have an interest in the plans to give their input, you are just two short steps away from securing their involvement on the fundraising team and their investment of a gift that will be at an appropriate level.

## Summary

- A resources study is a *qualitative* research process that identifies your organisation's readiness to mount a capital campaign and tests two vital fundraising resources: the source of contributable funds, and the volunteer workers who will become the champions to give and get them.
- Focus on converting the few that you need to give generously and avoid being paralysed into inactivity by those who fear change and fundraising.
- 80% of the fundraising target is raised from less than 20% of the total number of givers, with one gift in excess of 10% of the total amount secured.
- The three tools used in a resources study are the case statement, test scale of giving and quality interview list.
- The case statement must concisely tell a story which explains your:
  - reason for being
  - history
  - achievements
  - challenges
  - response
  - project benefits
  - cost breakdown
  - proposed fundraising methodology
  - pace-setting leadership
  - recognition
  - tax-effectiveness
  - vision for the future.
- When drawing-up a test scale of giving remember that:
  - most multi-million pound campaigns achieve 80% of their target from only 100–150 gifts, of which:
  - the top 10 gifts usually account for 45%–55% of the target, which would include:
  - the largest gift at normally 10%–15% of the amount to be raised.

- When developing a list of possible study interviewees, start by approaching your organisation's godparents, ask for their help to expand the interview list, to seek out the corners of your organisation's network, to speak to people who are probably just beyond the usual circle of current supporters. Aim to interview between 25 and 35 people.

**Capital Fundraising in the UK – the Compton Way**

# Chapter 4

# Identifying sources of funds: prospecting

Too often, important projects are shelved because of a misguided belief that the support of the whole community is necessary before mounting a capital fundraising campaign.

The majority of the wealth of this world is in the hands of a few, and large amounts of money can be raised if you focus on convincing the few to 'dig deep'. Concentrating your efforts on persuading a relatively small number of people to give generously to your project will significantly improve the chances of success.

## 80/20 rule (Pareto principle)

Capital fundraising campaigns achieve their goal with only a few hundred gifts. Invariably over 80% of the fundraising target is raised from less than 20% of the total number of givers, with one gift in excess of 10% of the full amount secured.

In other words, if you plan to raise £10 million, you should aim to achieve a top gift of at least £1 million.

## Types of gifts

Prospects become donors when they make a financial commitment to the fundraising campaign. Four different types of gift can be made, namely:

1. *Cash* – paid by cheque or direct bank transfer.
2. *Pledge* – a commitment to make a series of payments to the campaign over a period of time.
3. *Bequest* – a commitment to leave all or part of an estate to the campaign upon death.
4. *Gift-in-kind* – the contribution of needed goods or services.

All gifts of whatever type can only be included in the campaign total raised when they have been properly recorded. Written confirmation, either through the completion of a record card or letter is required to record a gift. Clearly a cheque, or the cash, is sufficient evidence for a cash gift.

In particular, it is important that all gifts-in-kind are professionally valued. In all cases, an appropriate external authority such as the project manager, quantity surveyor or other qualified person, should assess them.

## What is a prospect?

In short, a *prospect* is someone who has a known interest in your organisation or its work and the financial potential to make or influence a gift to your project at a level required by your scale of giving. Most importantly, you need genuine access to this person. (So, if you list Bill Gates as a prospect, make sure he'll return your call – or, at least, respond to your email!)

## Prospects not suspects

A *suspect* is someone with the potential to give, who might have a reason to be interested in your fundraising case statement and to whom you need to forge access. (We are often presented with various forms of published 'rich lists' in planning studies and campaigns and asked to take our pick of which prospects to approach first.)

Suspects can be converted to prospects as a campaign progresses. Mostly, though, our clients eventually accept the common sense of focusing on real prospects first. It is not surprising that those organisations that do this, significantly improve the chances of winning their campaign.

## Prospect development: the six Is

So who do we ask and for how much? The answer is not as difficult as some would lead you to believe and can be found by applying the following straightforward prospect development process:

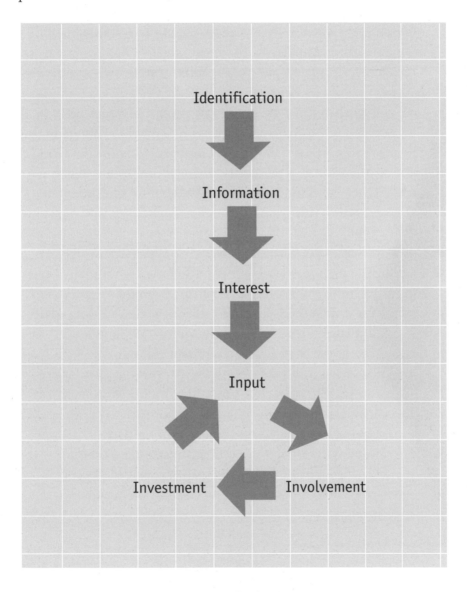

FIGURE 7: *Prospect development process*

FIG 7

If we pause for a moment and reflect, we know that:

- Identifying the names of wealthy people and then asking them for money does not work. Major gifts come from prospects that have a relationship with your organisation, at one level or another.
- Before a prospect is asked to make a major commitment, generally they need to know what is being asked of them and why their gift is important. The most effective way to do this is to make your prospect *part* of the cultivation process, a genuine partner.
- Once the gift is given, the engagement certainly does not stop. The next big gift is likely to come from a previous big giver. The more sophisticated the giver's understanding of the work of your organisation and the better the relationship, the more inclined they are going to be to make the next investment.

## 1 Identification

Begin by screening your list of suspects, to determine which are likely to be the major givers you need to win your campaign. Use a scoring system to help sort the prospects from the suspects. We review names against the following four categories, scoring each out of 25, so that those with the highest score are identified to progress through the prospect development process:

1.  *Capacity* – What indicators are there that this prospect has the means to be able to make a gift at the level being sought?
2.  *Propensity* – Has this prospect a track record of giving to your organisation, or other related fundraising initiatives?
3.  *Interest* – How interested in your organisation and the particular fundraising project is your prospect?
4.  *Access* – Who has a personal connection to the prospect and how strong is this?

| Prospect name | Capacity | Propensity | Interest | Access | Total |
|---|---|---|---|---|---|
| Mr Able Asker | 10 | 5 | 15 | 20 | **50** |
| Mrs Bet Bring | 20 | 20 | 15 | 15 | **70** |
| Mr Will Giver | 20 | 20 | 20 | 25 | **85** |
| Ms C.U. Later | 25 | 5 | 10 | 5 | **45** |

FIGURE 8: *Prospect screening sheet*

FIG 8

## Information

Once identified, next you must provide your prospects with an understanding of who you are and the vision behind your project. It's still not the time to talk about money. Specific information on your particular project must be provided in highly personalised ways, including personal invitations to tours, meetings with the chairman or chief executive or small, convivial social events at which presentations are made.

Your organisation's vision is central to the information presented. The big giver is not attracted by *need* but by innovation, aspiration and success. In many cases these days, the big giver is proving to be relatively young and entrepreneurial. We have found that his or her perspective as a giver is not dissimilar to that of a private investor.

## Interest

As this information is shared and these fundamental questions addressed, only then is the prospect ready to embark upon the final stages of the journey leading to the gift. By sharing information on your particular project you are able to explore what particular parts of it spark their interest. Now you can work to build this interest by addressing the benefits of the project and answering questions clearly and directly.

If what you want from them is money, to present your proposal at this stage may well be successful, but it's likely to elicit a token response. Once you have gained your prospect's interest in your project, you need to move on to build a genuine partnership by encouraging their input and involvement.

### **④⑤ Input and Involvement**

At this point we need to get creative. There's no 'one size fits all' strategy for managing how a prospect becomes involved with the organisation and starts to share its vision.

The approach must include legitimate opportunities to take in the prospect's views on the vision and for them to make, and be made to feel like they are making, substantive contributions to the process. Consider asking prospects to join advisory boards, project planning committees, to become engaged in interface with Government or suppliers – or believe it or not – to fundraise.

### **⑥ Investment**

At this stage in the prospect development process, the idea of giving is the logical next step, for your prospect as well as the asker. If, when the time comes to ask for the gift, your prospect is surprised, you haven't done your homework.

### **Relationship cycle**

The gift triggers the start of the continuous relationship cycle: the structured format by which you plan to demonstrate how seriously you take the relationship. It begins with the obvious: thanks and acknowledgement from the highest levels of the organisation, but it also takes a new way of looking at the organisation.

We have seen major givers completing their pledges, become even more deeply associated with the organisation (through board membership, volunteer fundraising or even just regularly diarised meetings with senior officials), and then present fresh, innovative ideas, in line with the institutional priorities, which they are prepared to fund. In effect, when the relationship cycle has been managed properly, these organisations have found themselves in the enviable position of the reverse ask: 'Here's a proposal I have to put to you. Will you consider implementing it and consider letting me fund it?'

## No magic wand: and few surprises

Contrary to popular opinion, until we have conducted a resources study, fundraising consultants probably have even less of an idea of where the money is to come from than you do. However, with 40 years of fundraising experience under our belts, we are probably going to look a little dismayed if you suggest that the top gift on your scale of giving might come from the Sultan of Brunei, or others who regularly appear at the top of the published wealth lists.

At the risk of repeating ourselves, we hold a passionate belief that capital fundraising is organised common sense. In the main, financial commitments to capital projects and programmes come from thoroughly predictable sources.

Your real prospects are your closest friends, board members, previous givers, supporters, stakeholders and volunteer workers – and, of course, if you manage a really good campaign, the closest friends of your closest friends.

With this in mind, nominating the right group of interviewees for the resources study (based on a combination of *influence* and *affluence*) is crucial. We are inevitably posed the question: *'Where do we find such people?'*

## Face reality: don't make excuses

It can be difficult to face up to the way things *really* are. Organisations get nervous about targeting their close friends for a fundraising campaign. They fear that this will destroy the great goodwill that has been carefully cultivated through their *friend raising*. We are often told that:

- focusing on eminent volunteers who are already giving their time to the organisation is wrong.
- an organisation's 'consumers' are already paying for services and shouldn't be bothered by fundraisers.

We are often on the receiving end of sermons about how *unethical* it is to approach one's closest friends and associates for money – to say nothing of those organisations that have an 'ethos' (we could have devoted an entire chapter to this) which would be destroyed by fundraising. Finally, failing all else, there is always the ultimate position that person-to-person solicitation for funds is all rather 'distasteful and vulgar'.

### We know it's not easy, but ...

We understand these objections. Capital fundraising may well be common sense, but it is not easy. We know how hard it can be to nominate a close friend as a prospect for a fundraising campaign. We too treasure the 'social capital' of organisations (and are usually the ones who highlight the value of this intangible asset to our clients).

Most of the time, the reluctance to nominate real prospects is created by a fear of personal giving and the thought of, ultimately, having to ask friends and associates for money. Again, this is understandable but the truth of the matter is that if you want to raise big money, you have to focus on your friends first. Remember, your fundraising resources study is built around a group of your institutional 'godparents'. In fundraising jargon: your inner 'constituency circle'.

One of the most common reasons why we are commissioned to conduct resources studies is that, as objective outsiders, we can ask difficult questions of your closest friends and volunteer leaders. You must involve these people in researching and planning your capital campaign. They will invariably have the access to the *influence* and *affluence* you need to attain your financial goal. Furthermore, and ironically, if you do not seek their input, you run a real risk of losing their friendship and support.

## Prospect sources: a checklist

So, where do prospects come from? Review the following checklist and see how many of the categories apply to your campaign. Then put the 'rich lists' back on your shelf and focus on your *real* friends and prospects.

**FIG 9**

| Your board members | Must be involved in your capital campaign as givers and, ideally, askers. |
|---|---|
| Your board's contacts | Who do your board members know? |
| Previous givers | As unfair as it might seem, they are your best source of future prospects. |
| Friends of previous givers | Many of your best prospects are under your very nose. A well-planned and managed 'Giver Refer Prospect' process will reveal them to you. |
| Patrons | If you have them, you've probably asked them to do nothing but 'lend their name' to your cause. If asked, they will often do much more. |
| Ex-board members | If they are still happy to talk to you – pick their brains. |
| Key members of your management team | We all know someone with money or access to it. |
| Other staff members | Members of your institutional 'family' should be consulted early. |
| Your clients, stakeholders, consumers, users | Whatever you call them. Whether they are parents, students, patients or visitors – consult them. Treat them as 'stakeholders' and not merely 'consumers' paying a fee for a service. Ask them who they know. |
| Alumni groups | This doesn't just apply to schools, colleges and universities. Keep track of all of those people whose lives are touched by your organisation. The networks they offer could well be the ones that win your campaign. |

| Friends groups | If you are lucky enough to have an organisation with structured groups of volunteers, make sure you seek their input early on. |
| --- | --- |
| Suppliers | Don't just ask them for money – ask them to open their networks to you. |
| Neighbours | Individuals, companies and other organisations. Think about the social and economic impact you have on your locale. Can this be used to advance your campaign? |
| Corporate contacts | Local businesses, chambers of commerce, regional companies, national corporations and even multi-nationals. Again, who do you know? Can you respond to the inevitable 'What's in it for us' question? |
| Grant-making trusts | They exist purely to give money away. There are some 9,000 trusts in the UK making grants of £2 billion a year. Again, who do you know who can guide you through the guidelines and application procedures? |
| Government/quasi-Government funding | If you are happy to accept it and your project hits the right political buttons:<br>• Lottery funding    • Local government<br>• Landfill tax    • Regional development funds<br>• European funding<br><br>An hour with your MEP is often more valuable than a guru with a friend in Brussels. |
| Community service organisations | Rotary, Lions, Round Table and others with discretionary grant-making powers and powerful volunteer networks. |
| Other charitable organisations | Are there other not-for-profits with funds to allocate for the particular project you are championing? Are there strategic alliance/funding opportunities? |
| Others nominated by study interviewees | Remember to ask that final question of your study interviewees: 'Who else should we talk to?' |
| The grass roots community | At the right time, in the right way, how are you going to make your campaign inclusive through a bolt-on, broader-based 'appeal' or survey? |

## Prospect identification and listing

In some cases (for example, schools, churches and sports clubs) there is a readily identifiable, closed constituency of prospects, where it is possible to list the details of every potential giver. Other organisations have open constituencies – and more work needs to be put in to get answers to the questions of who will support you and why – still, in most settings, it is possible to identify a preliminary 'flat list' of suspects and prospects for further investigation.

### Prospect evaluation: screening and rating

You can build all the lists in the world, but without some kind of evaluation process they are useless. You simply must ask some basic questions about your prospective support base:

- *Screening* – Do they have the potential to give to your fundraising campaign – capacity, prosperity, interest and access? (See Figure 8, page 55.)
- *Rating* – What do you think they will give if asked by the right person, at the right time, in the right place for the right part of the project?

Prospect screening generates ballpark figures and ranges of prospective giving for further exploration. Prospect *rating* offers a 'think about' figure for a visitor to take to a prospect.

### How to conduct prospect evaluation

There are two main ways to build up an evaluated prospect list:

1. *Prospect review committee* – a group of knowledgeable volunteers who meet in a confidential setting with the preliminary 'flat list' to give their thoughts on particular prospects (be they individuals, families, corporations, statutory funds or grant-making trusts).
2. *Personal prospect review* – the 'think about' figure listed by the volunteer who nominated the prospect in the first place as a friend, associate or a 'peer'.

There is much debate about which of these evaluation procedures works best. Should you spend vast amounts of time researching *Who's Who* and forming prospect review committees to refine the ever-growing lists? Should you accept the fact that some of your prospects are already sufficiently *cultivated* for you to be able to ask them for their input to a resources study – or even ask them for money – and be able to identify like-minded peers who could do the same? We favour the latter strategy, but it does no harm to combine these techniques to ensure full coverage of your constituency.

### What prospect evaluation is not

Some agencies trade in wealth 'research'. Give them access to your database (a risky proposition in its own right), and they will highlight where they suspect the wealth may be. This might (if you are very lucky) highlight giving potential. You still have to establish access and interest to such suspects and you've spent a few thousand pounds along the way.

Other firms trade in information they have gathered from confidential fundraising studies and giving to campaigns they have managed for other clients. This is poor ethics, we suggest (confirmed as such by our industry's code of practice). Furthermore, it's an ineffective strategy. We've seen endless reports of this type (lists of wealthy givers) gathering dust on shelves. They are not actionable. After all, why should giving to one project automatically translate to another?

Do not waste time, money and your social capital by taking the path of least resistance. Consult your 'champions'. Find out who you know and what they might be worth to your campaign by talking to those 'insiders' who really know the score.

### Why prospect evaluation is so important

What everyone appears to agree on is that there has been precious little quality prospect review of any kind in recent years in the UK. Generally, capital campaign performance has suffered as a result of this.

As hard as it might be to talk about other people's money, prospect evaluation is crucial for two main reasons:

- *In the resources study* – if you don't ask these questions, how do you confirm the feasibility of your funding plans and scenarios? Without quality review of the scale of giving with those 'in the know', you cannot win your campaign on paper. You will be shooting in the dark.
- *In the campaign* – prospective givers almost always want to know what is expected of them. You will need to ask for a specific range or amount.

Do not dodge prospect screening and rating. You will not be successful without it. In capital fundraising, money flows to power and influence. Ask yourself – who do you know of power and influence – or access to these qualities? Then ask yourself – how do you reach out to them?

## Summary

- Generally, major gifts to capital campaigns come from predictable sources.
- Focus on your closest 'friends' first.
- List 'real' prospects (not suspects from the rich list) each of which has a known interest, clear giving potential, a propensity to give and with whom you have some level of personal access.
- Classify and evaluate your prospects through some form of prospect evaluation to 'win your campaign on paper'.

# Chapter 5

# The campaign plan

## Success is 80% planning

In capital fundraising, as with many other ventures, success is 80% planning.

As outlined in previous chapters of this book, let's assume that:

- Your organisation has done its quantitative and qualitative research in the form of a resources study.
- There is an institutional development plan that clearly highlights where projects and programmes fit into future strategy.
- There is broad consensus throughout the organisation (led by the governing body) that the capital project is urgent, compelling and the right way to proceed.
- The project, and its impact on operational programmes and funding, has been sensibly costed.
- Your organisation has been in some sort of dialogue with its stakeholder groups (who should be treated as partners and not just periodic donors or consumers).
- Some thought has been given as to how the level of funding needed might be broken down and cash flowed across the different funding sources and audiences to which your organisation and its fundraisers have access.

## The written fundraising plan

With these elements of success in place, it is time to bring them to life in the form of a written fundraising plan. So, what should be included in our fundraising 'road map'?

## Where to start:

Review and consideration of the following, 14-point framework could be useful:

1. **The fundraising 'case statement': who are you and why do you need the money?**

   To begin, re-state with confidence, clarity and enthusiasm why you need to raise the money. This case statement is your fundraising story – and it should be exactly that: a narrative that flows with ease, because it is a story that will be told time and time again (hopefully, with passion and consistency) by board members, volunteer fundraisers and professional fundraising staff.

   Articulate your financial goals with certainty and talk about these goals as *opportunities* rather than burdens – using the language of *investment* rather than the begging bowl.

2. **The ethos issue: your attitude towards person-to-person fundraising**

   We know that successful major gifts fundraising is based on well-trained and supported volunteers making personal approaches.

   Unfortunately, experience suggests that there is no plan B – so it is vital that the concept of volunteer-led, professionally managed fundraising is embraced with enthusiasm.

   While the concept of building and supporting a network of givers and askers might, on the face of it, look daunting, your time, work and resources will be well spent. And, if you examine the origins of your charity, organisation or movement – the chances are you will find that a few committed people who got together to give time and money to the cause or vision formed it.

Yet, a remarkable number of organisations try to use 'institutional ethos' as an excuse for not adopting person-to-person fundraising methodology.

The fact is that you simply must find the institutional courage to face up to the reality that big money needs to be asked for person-to-person. So, rather than reluctant acceptance of face-to-face, peer-to-peer solicitation for funds, why not state – right up front in the campaign plan – why this fundraising methodology is right for your organisation and how you intend to use it to involve your stakeholders in the project and raise 'social capital' as well as big money.

### 3. Principles of capital fundraising

With the ethos battle won, you can then address the 12 key principles of capital fundraising, and how you intend to make them work for you. A tip for fundraising managers: *know the principles off by heart*. They will serve you well.

If you can't remember them: we have included them again as Figure 10 overleaf. Copy them on to an index card or hand-held computer device and carry them with you.

| | |
|---|---|
| **1.** | Leadership by example is the most important feature of a successful campaign. We cannot expect someone to do what we are not prepared to do ourselves. |
| **2.** | Every member of the governing body and the fundraising leadership group must give as generously as they can. Their leadership gifts will be a major factor in raising the sights of other givers to the project. |
| **3.** | People rarely give to causes. They give to people with causes. |
| **4.** | Prospective givers must be able to place their trust in the honesty and integrity of the institution involved. |
| **5.** | Prospective givers should always be approached face-to-face. Only when asked clearly and directly, will they want to make a generous gift. |
| **6.** | Prospective givers will be strongly influenced by someone they know and respect – and someone who has already given. |
| **7.** | People like to know what is expected of them. In asking for a gift, members of the fundraising team should clearly indicate the level of support being sought. |
| **8.** | Team members will usually obtain gifts of a similar size, or commitment, to their own. |
| **9.** | People will often be persuaded to give more, when they are motivated by appropriate forms of recognition. |
| **10.** | Prospective givers will be encouraged to raise their sights, when given the opportunity to pledge contributions over a period of time. |
| **11.** | Publicity will help create the right climate for fundraising, but will not in itself, generally, raise money. |
| **12.** | Campaigns that show early signs of success usually go on to achieve their target. |

FIGURE 10: *Twelve principles of capital fundraising*

**FIG 10**

### 4. Where is the money coming from? Targeted sources and audiences

Of course, the plan can only really be shaped when you know where you hope to get the money from. Your resources study should have identified sources of prospective givers and leaders – and how their activities on your behalf will be

**Capital Fundraising in the UK – the Compton Way**

geared across approaches to individual benefactors, grant-making trusts, corporate givers and broader-based community supporters.

You need to articulate who you are going to approach, when, for how much, for which part of your project and why.

5.  **The scale of giving. How is the fundraising goal broken down?**
    The scale of giving (the number of pledges needed at different levels to reach the goal) follows naturally from the section on targeted prospects.

    The scale will have been revised in the resources study and will be fine-tuned throughout the campaign – as you constantly evaluate the potential and prospective givers and endeavour to match streams of potential resources to streams of opportunities.

6.  **Campaign organisational chart**
    Who's going to do the work? To whom are they accountable? How will the capital campaign fit in to your ongoing, annual fundraising plans? Where do your board and in-house management team fit in?

    A user-friendly organisational chart should map this out and confirm exactly who's supposed to be doing what. (See Chapter 7 on organising volunteers for an example.) If there is one page of the campaign plan that can summarise the job to be done, it is probably the organisational chart (see Figure 12, page 102).

7.  **Job descriptions**
    As a second insurance policy against confusion of roles, get written job description summaries into your fundraising plan: for board members, volunteer leaders, management team members and all staff associated with fundraising in your organisation.

    Remember to keep it simple. Yes, individual volunteers will operate in different sectors. Some will be better at individual rather than corporate approaches, for example but, in short, we want volunteers to:

- make thoughtful and proportionate financial commitments (usually spread over a 3–5-year pledge period) to the project
- make a list of personal prospects whom they feel they could approach for money
- work with the campaign manager to get ready to make the approach
- ask these genuine, listed prospects personally (when ready) to support the campaign.

8. **Communications and fundraising tools**

Your volunteer team will need promotional props. What fundraising and communications tools do you plan to have at their disposal? As outlined in more detail in Chapter 11, probably combinations of the following:

- a campaign brochure (a more visual, user-friendly rendition of the case statement)
- an artist's impression of the project (or some other graphic visualisation of the work to be done if you are not campaigning for bricks and mortar)
- 'ways of giving' documentation
- a list of giving and recognition opportunities
- gift and pledge forms
- Frequently Asked Questions (FAQ sheet)
- CD-ROM (a visual, animated version of the case statement)
- PowerPoint and other forms of visual presentations
- written proposals
- dedicated campaign stationery linked to your campaign 'theme' or 'brand'
- a guide/support kit for your volunteer fundraising team members.

You need to know why you are spending money, and be convinced that it's the right promotional tool for the job; remembering the fundamental principle that publicity, in its own right, does not raise money.

9. **Tax-effective giving**

It has never been easier and as tax-effective to be generous to charitable causes in the UK, and details and illustrations of tax-effective, 'ways of giving' should be included in your fundraising plan.

10. **Donor acknowledgement, recognition and communication**

You should know, in detail, what happens to money and associated paperwork (and information) when it arrives in your organisation. How are gifts and pledges recorded, processed, acknowledged and reported? How do you plan to recognise donors and sponsors? A brief, written policy document on recognition is always a good idea. What ongoing communications will givers receive to let them know that their money is being well spent? Many organisations seem to think that fundraising stops when the money is received when, in fact, the job of saying thank you to givers, and building ongoing relationships with them has only just started.

11. **Managing your resources: the campaign operational budget**

If your resources study has shown that you need to plan and manage, maybe, less than 100 high-level personal approaches – you do not need to spend thousands of pounds on brochures. If your audience of prospective givers all live within a local catchment area, it is unlikely that you'll be spending vast amounts of money to reach them (distinct from nationwide campaigns, where travel, accommodation and communication costs might be much more significant).

Spend enough to set up and properly manage your campaign (as under investment is a major inhibitor to capital fundraising) but gear your operational budget to the shape and realities of your campaign logistics – and spend and monitor it wisely.

What needs to be spent and where will depend on the particular nature of your organisation and its needs but, as a rule of thumb, campaign operational budgets can be drafted on the 1/3, 1/3, 1/3 guideline in which:

- 1/3 of the budget is allocated to campaign office administrative support (usually a dedicated office manager or personal assistant)
- 1/3 to promotional materials and campaign marketing
- 1/3 to campaign office infrastructure (office space and equipment).

Remember, industry standards in the UK indicate that it is reasonable to invest anything from 5%–15% of the target in fees and costs in order to successfully manage a capital campaign.

### 12. Monitoring progress: campaign reporting

As detailed in Chapter 10, fundraising should be one of the most measurable fields of activity – yet many organisations find it difficult to keep track of how much money has been raised in pledges, what the campaign's cash flow is like and how much potential is still out there in pending and yet to be delivered proposals.

Again, set the right expectations. Let boards and management teams know how you are going to report: on a weekly, monthly and quarterly basis. Reporting is much easier if you have a fundraising database (or customised reports from it) that is linked to fundraising performance against your scale of giving.

Where are the timing issues, soft spots and other variations? Be confident about your targets (that includes, on occasions, the confidence to state why they have been re-forecasted or missed).

### 13. Fundraising timetable

Capital campaigns are intensive. This needs to be emphasised in the timetable, as the busy and influential volunteers who are key to their success will tend not to sign up for an indefinite period of activity: they will be used to deadlines.

Give your organisation those deadlines. Begin with the broad phases of activity; break these down further into monthly goals and, as the campaign progresses, weekly and daily objectives. (See Figure 11, page 76.)

Above all else, without prose and chart timetables, how can you guarantee that you do not miss crucial fundraising deadlines and donor expectations?

## 14. Conclusion: visionary call to action from your campaign leader

It is important that your volunteer campaign leader signs the plan and concludes it with a rousing, 'big picture' statement of intent and call for action. This nails the volunteer ownership of the campaign to the mast and sets the tone for the spirit of the campaign.

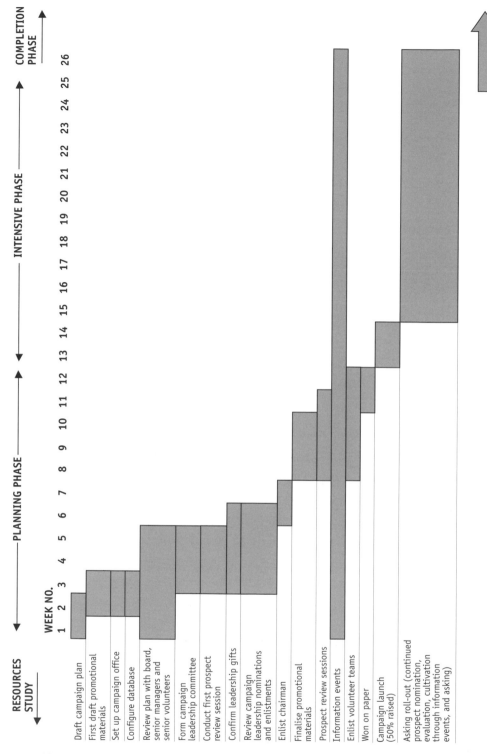

FIGURE 11: *Outline campaign timetable for a 26-week school fundraising campaign*

FIG 11

## So, whose plan is it anyway?

If a campaign plan is to be meaningful and actionable, it needs to belong to everyone in your organisation, as, particularly in a capital campaign, fundraising needs to become a little part of everyone's job.

A well-planned and managed campaign should engage the board, senior management, employees, friends, suppliers, neighbours, and, most importantly, your various networks of volunteers and prospective donors.

## What is the plan used for?

The fundraising plan is your blueprint for fundraising success. It should help you to reduce the many risks involved in capital fundraising:

- Who is to be asked for money?
- By whom?
- Where?
- When?
- For how much?
- For what part of the project?

The written plan should help you to avoid the worst of the uncertainty and complexity that can plague campaigns, but the plan's no good to anyone if it merely stays on your shelf or in a drawer.

## Use the plan to:

- **focus** your board and management leadership on what is required of them and the organisation as a whole
- **enlist** quality volunteers to your fundraising teams and keep them 'on message'
- **make sure** that your organisation's investment in fundraising is sufficient and is yielding an acceptable return.

## Fundraising priorities

Finally, use the campaign plan to get your priorities right and to help you to properly value your time. A good plan will help you to recognise the difference between what you are comfortable doing (which may have little impact on fundraising success) and those issues and situations which may be more challenging but, if approached in a direct and professional way, will generate the best fundraising performance from your board, management and volunteer team.

## No written plan: failure factors

When capital fundraising campaigns go wrong – they tend to do so with a long whimper rather than a big bang. Capital campaigns involve your key leaders and major prospective supporters and can be incredibly damaging to institutional and personal reputations if they go wrong.

Failing campaigns tend to get slowly but surely bogged down in a mire of complexity and uncertainty – a thick and particularly sticky mud of institutional denial, abdication of responsibility, selective memory of who was supposed to do what and, ultimately – blame.

Invariably, failing campaigns are found to have no actionable written plan: no 'road map' to, at least, guide institutional leaders, staff and volunteers in the right direction; to provide a reference point for where the campaign lost its way and how it can get back on track.

And, if you recognise any of the following comments or reactions, beware – because they are usually early indicators of looming failure.

### Beware ...

*'We're different ... it would be against our ethos to ask people for money.'*

*'If we ask people for money they will be irritated and we'll lose their support.'*

*'All we need to do is ask one million people to give us £1 each.'*

*'We need to spend money on a nice brochure and mail it to everyone on our database.'*

'We need a high profile celebrity patron.'

'We can't ask people for money unless we launch a big advertising campaign first.'

'Our paid fundraising staff should ask for the money — not our board members.'

'I give my time, I shouldn't also be expected to give my money.'

'We shouldn't spend money on fundraising — we're a charity and people should do things for us for nothing.'

'We can't approach our donors — they've already been so generous. You can't keep going back to the well.'

'We won't raise big money without a big event.'

'Why are we spending so much time on a campaign plan? Let's just go and do it.'

## Summary

1. Complexity and uncertainty will kill a capital fundraising project.

2. 80% of fundraising success is in the planning phase.

3. Know the 'anatomy' of a written fundraising plan. It will, at least, tell you where things are going wrong and, possibly, save you from the institutional embarrassment of a failed capital campaign:

   - who are you, what do you do and why do you need the money: *case statement*
   - your institutional ethos: why you are adopting person-to-person fundraising methodology
   - the principles of capital fundraising
   - where is the money coming from: *target audiences*
   - how is the fundraising goal broken down: *scale of giving*
   - how will you line up and manage your human resources: *campaign organisational chart*
   - what do you want people to do: *job and task descriptions*
   - communications and fundraising tools
   - confirmation of tax-effective giving
   - donor acknowledgement, recognition and ongoing communication
   - managing your financial investment: *campaign operational budget*
   - monitoring progress and return on investment: *campaign reporting*
   - deadline-driven timetable
   - conclusion: *inspiring statement of intent from your volunteer campaign leader* 'Why I have given and want you to do the same.'

# Chapter 6

# Leadership is everything

## Volunteer leadership

### The key to successful capital fundraising

Many years of planning and managing capital campaigns have taught us that volunteer leadership is the most important factor in successful 'big gift' fundraising.

Money flows to *power* and *influence*.

So, if your not-for-profit organisation wants to raise a significant amount of money for a special project or programme, you will need to have the volunteer leadership power for the job.

### Other success factors

✓ Yes, of course. Your fundraising 'case for support' needs to be urgent and compelling.

✓ Yes, the political, financial and operational thinking behind your project needs to stack up.

✓ Yes, you need to identify an appropriate pool of prospective past givers and new financial supporters.

✓ Yes, you need capable fundraising managers.

✓ Yes, you need a good fundraising database.

✓ And, yes, campaign marketing and promotional tools should be fresh and appealing.

### But where's the clout?

Even with all these other success factors in place, without an influential volunteer leader, you will not see a full return on your fundraising investment.

Copies of the latest rich lists; textbook fundraising policies and procedures and a growing, pleasant team of 'friend-raisers' running endless events is one thing – but, without leadership clout of *influence* and *affluence*, you will not achieve your organisation's major gift potential. You will leave money on the table: because major gifts are only secured through the skilful application of 'peer-to-peer' leverage.

### The star player

Why do some 'premier league' not-for-profits with great projects fail to reach their capital fundraising goals? Yet, at the same time many seemingly 'lower division' charities with limited profile and resources, or new organisations obviously punching way above their weight, enjoy tremendous capital fundraising success? Take a closer look and you'll find a powerful, volunteer fundraising leader – a star player – behind the success stories.

### Characteristics of a fundraising chairman

Fundraising chairmen (male and female) come in all sorts of shapes and sizes – and from all kinds of backgrounds. However, there are common denominators that have been documented ad nauseam by dozens of fundraisers over the last century (including three or four generations of Compton consultants).

The fundraising chairman must be committed to the cause, and:
- take responsibility for meeting or exceeding the campaign objective
- not countenance failure
- be regarded as prominent, respected, capable, knowledgeable and well connected
- have political, economic or social power and leverage, and be willing to pull these levers to pave the way and ask for major gifts

- be capable of a substantial gift (this is vital) and should be one of the first people to make a financial pledge
- be able to recruit a team of fundraising sub-chairmen
- put his/her reputation on the line by being ready and willing to become the public spokesperson for the campaign.

**Our recent experience ...**
Current and recent experience would lead us to add the following traits to the leadership requirements list.

A successful fundraising chairman:

✓ is likely to still be active in high-level business life at board level
✓ will have a track record of community service or interest in philanthropy
✓ will be busy, demanding, used to success and occasionally impatient
✓ will have used your organisation's services or be interested in your area of work
✓ will, usually, be known to one of your governing body, senior management team, major donors or other volunteer supporters
✓ will be prepared to ask for money (on a person-to-person basis) and will relate to direct networking fundraising principles and practice because of involvement in high-level sales or marketing activity
✓ will (despite previous experience of personal fundraising and business experience) still ask for guidance and counsel on what needs to be done.

**So, what do we want the fundraising chairman to do?**
Our experience suggests that busy, influential people like to keep things simple, so here is what we ask of fundraising chairmen on Compton-managed campaigns:

✓ make a major financial commitment to the project
✓ work with 'us' (including the board and the senior management team of the client organisation) to help identify

and close the top 10 or 20 fundraising approaches needed to win the campaign

✓ help us to enlist a team of powerful fundraising volunteers to expand the fundraising network and open more doors to prospective givers

✓ maintain close liaison with the board and management of the not-for-profit and become the key spokesman for the fundraising campaign.

### Where do we find such leaders?

As outlined in Chapter 3, no major fundraising project or programme should proceed without a 'resources study' to identify sources of volunteer leadership as well as sources of funding. Your study should identify candidates for the position of fundraising chairman – or networks that will lead you to such candidates. The majority of fundraising leaders are known to board members or other institutional godparents and these institutional influencers should all be consulted in this first, critical piece of planning work.

### Not the 'usual suspects'

Re-shuffled 'usual suspect' wealth lists from newspapers or so-called special 'profiles' from list and research agencies will not, generally, help you to identify your campaign leader. Again, we need to emphasise that, in our experience, it is rare to identify and enlist an entirely 'external' campaign leader.

You need to find someone known to you and who has genuine access to the kind of person who can genuinely play the key role of the fundraising chairman.

Such leaders are priceless. For any given fundraising campaign, in any town, city or region, there may only be two or three qualified leadership candidates. You have to ensure that you get one of them to do the job.

### Cultivating the prospective chairman: softly but surely

Ultimately, 'we need you' are the golden words of leadership enlistment. However, a good deal of *cultivation* may be required over several visits before you are in a position to make the proposition.

Tread softly but surely. This quality person is a rare resource. Patiently nudge the enlistment process forward. Play to the candidate's timetable, not just the needs of your project. Be prepared to answer the increasingly detailed questions about your organisation's mission, ethos, governance, management and financial position. And be prepared to make the 'Ask' – when the time is right.

**When is the right time to enlist the campaign chairman?**
Ideally, someone on the charity's governing body, or close to it, is identified in the study and agrees to do the job as part of the study interview, report and presentation process. So, generally always, the earlier the better.

However, real life seldom works this way and leaders are targeted and enlisted at all stages of fundraising campaigns.

In fact, sometimes it can pay to wait for the right campaign chairman. Maybe the candidate's personal or business commitments mean that the leader will have to be phased into the campaign. Maybe the advice you have is that momentum has to be built a little more before you formally approach the prospective leader. Maybe no real leadership candidates have yet emerged and your organisation has to demonstrate self-help leadership success first as part of the process of attracting a targeted leader.

Good timing can be crucial to getting the right person. Do not tap dance around a good candidate who's ready to be asked ... but don't be too concerned about waiting for the right person and the right time: as long as your board or fundraising leadership committee is bridging the gap as well as possible in the meantime.

**Making the enlistment 'Ask'**
When the time comes, be prepared to answer the following questions:

*'What do you want me to do?'*

*'How much time is it going to take?'*

'What support will your organisation give me?'

And, when the time comes, don't fudge the answers:

'We want a campaign leader who will help us to raise our financial goal by giving money and asking others to do the same – at the major levels needed to make the project a success.'

'The job is task rather than time-driven, but will still take 4–5 hours a week during the intensive phase of the campaign.'

'You'll be working in partnership with our board, management and fundraising team. We've set up a dedicated fundraising office and experienced, quality fundraisers will be on hand to work with you on this special project which is our greatest institutional priority.'

### Meeting the chairman's demands: question time

Before your leadership candidate agrees to accept the role of fundraising chairman, he or she will undertake the due diligence involved. Here are just some of the questions our clients and Compton consultants have faced in enlisting the right chairman:

'Why are you asking me to do this?'

'Has this project been fully agreed by your board and staff? Is everyone behind it?'

'Are you sure that the project costs are correct – and will remain so?'

'Have you raised big money before? What makes you so sure you can do it now?'

'How have you arrived at your fundraising goal?'

'Did you conduct a fundraising resources study?'

'Is your ongoing financial position strong enough to sustain the annual, operating costs of this capital project?'

'How will raised funds be managed?'

'Have your board members made their own financial commitments to this project?'

'Are you undertaking any other fundraising apart from this? If so, for what and who's being targeted?'

'Do you have a written fundraising plan for the campaign?'

'What about the marketing plan for the campaign?'

'Has your fundraising team got the resources and experience to do the job you're asking of them (that is, give me the quality support I'll need)?'

'If I don't agree to do this — what will you do?'

'What's the worst thing that could happen to me if I agree to do this?'

## Success factors ...

Our early advice to an incoming chairman of a capital fundraising campaign is to focus on the following 'markers' that will ensure their campaign is a success:

✓ Conduct one-on-one (or two-on-one) personal, face-to-face approaches to recruit other volunteers or to ask for gifts.
✓ Get your largest gifts first — to 'benchmark' the campaign — to raise the giving sights of others and to secure substantial challenge gifts, if possible.
✓ Ask those people who know you best to give the most and soonest.
✓ Keep it clear and simple by always asking your prospect to take on a clearly defined volunteer role or for a specific amount or range of gift.

## Guaranteed failure

Equally, there are a number of failure indicators that a prospective fundraising chairman should heed (and we hope that your organisation is not familiar with them):

*'Of course, we only want to use your name for our appeal letter.'*

*'It won't take much time ... you'll just have to sign a few letters.'*

*'It's an honorary position ... not an executive, working role.'*

*'We don't want you to ask for money ... our professional fundraisers will do all of the asking.'*

*'We only want a token gift from you as you are being so generous with your time.'*

## The wealth question

One of the questions we are most often asked is whether or not a volunteer leader without personal big gift potential can successfully chair a major fundraising campaign? The answer is yes – it has happened and doubtless, it will happen again. However, statistics rather than merely dogma support our assertion that this case is the exception rather than the rule. If considering this approach to fundraising leadership, it is worth asking one central question:

*'Is your organisation and the prospective fundraising leader that exceptional that you can afford to break one of the golden rules of fundraising?'*

## Getting what you deserve

One of the most memorable advertising straplines of all time was for a well-known leadership development course:

*'You don't get the deal you deserve ... you get the deal you negotiate.'*

If you lose your nerve when your rare prospective leader asks you the key questions, you will get what you deserve: opportunity loss and fundraising failure.

If, on the other hand, you rise to the challenge of enlisting a busy, powerful, wealthy and influential volunteer chairman; your fundraising campaign is already half-won.

## Summary

- Money flows to power and influence. Strong volunteer leadership is the most important success factor in capital fundraising.
- Successful fundraising campaign chairmen make big gifts themselves and help to identify and secure the 'Top 10 or 20' pledges needed on the scale of giving.
- It is rare to find an 'external' campaign leader.
- Be prepared to answer these key, leadership enlistment questions:
  - What do you want me to do?
  - How much time is it going to take?
  - What support will your organisation give me?

*Do not lose your nerve. Ask your prospective fundraising chairman to provide the leadership you really need.*

# Chapter 7

# Volunteers have the power: organising the campaign

## Organising your fundraising network

Fundraising staff who are paid for their time and talents, no matter how enthusiastic and dedicated they are, do not have the same 'asking power' as a volunteer who is leading by example.

Many of the largest and most challenging fundraising campaigns being run in the UK today are led by a handful of dedicated volunteers who are using their influence and affluence to raise millions of pounds.

Who you choose to be the volunteer leaders of your campaign will be the single most important decision you make and will have a major impact on the amount of money raised. We know those who agree to give and ask others to join them as 'visitors', to distinguish these key people from other volunteers. The name also reinforces the way that visitors have decided to raise money – through personal approaches asking prospects they know for gifts to the campaign.

To make the most of the volunteer resources available to your organisation, you will need a first-rate professional: a campaign manager. He or she will work in partnership with your volunteer leadership applying the skills required to identify, enlist and train the visitors. (See Chapter 6 for more detail.) An experienced campaign manager is a key asset in persuading busy volunteers to take on the responsibility of leading a campaign, so make sure you resource this vital role appropriately.

## Managing visitors

The campaign manager will ensure that visitors are assigned to the right prospects. In addition, he or she will give all volunteers the skills required through training and close mentoring, to deliver higher levels of performance.

The campaign manager must be an excellent time manager. Working to a tight timetable he or she will take care to use volunteer time judiciously, while creating a genuine sense of urgency and momentum for the conduct of the campaign.

Managing volunteers is less about 'direction' and command and control management techniques, and more about the use of softer, intuitive skills of persuasion to get the most out of busy and influential people.

### Tips for effective campaign managers

Campaign managers use the following 'tips' when managing visitors:

1. Before the first meeting with a visitor, do some research. Find out what you can about the visitor's relationship with the organisation, record of previous giving and personal background.

2. When you meet, remember that first impressions count. Be punctual and presentable. Avoid appearing too different – people are more comfortable with those who seem similar to them.

3. Respect the visitor's time. Work to a written agenda: tick off items as they are completed. Take notes openly. Ask what is the best time, place and form for all future communication with the visitor.

4. Create a sense of urgency. At the end of the meeting:
   • Confirm who will do what next.
   • Agree the purpose of the next meeting, and then make the arrangements.

5. Within 24 hours provide action-focused notes of the meeting (not extensive minutes). Be prompt in all routine contact with the visitor, courteously delivering what is promised on time and to a professional standard. Avoid 'snowing' the visitor with rafts of paper: provide bullet-point summaries. Brevity and clarity are vital.

6. Never reject out of hand the suggestion of a visitor. If the idea is of questionable value, simply indicate that you would like to consider it further. Then examine the suggestion to see if something worthwhile can be found. This will save face for the visitor and allow time to consider the idea. The key is to ensure that the visitor takes 'ownership' of the campaign, not the campaign manager.

7. Do not be an expert. Be candid. Be professional, but be ready to 'lose a few battles to win the war'. No one likes someone who knows it all. So try and build up your visitors so they become the fundraising *experts*.

## Briefing visitors

The first place to start is to ensure that all volunteers understand what is being asked of them to help win the campaign. This is best achieved through a formal briefing process.

Briefing of the volunteer team will be a continuous activity throughout all phases of the campaign with each meeting designed to enhance and develop the team's ability to achieve success.

Campaign managers may find it necessary to brief visitors on an individual basis and the same principles will apply as for a group briefing.

A typical briefing will consist of these features:
- a report on the continuing success of the campaign by the campaign manager or the team leader
- a project information update

- a discussion on the scale of giving
- a review of prospect listing
- an in-depth discussion on the principles of fundraising
- an asking briefing: five steps to success
- a role play of a fundraising visit
- an agreement on deadlines ahead.

Experience has shown that it is best to complete the briefing during one meeting, but if necessary it can be handled over two.

Care should be taken with the following:

1. A visitor should not be allocated prospects until he or she has made a personal gift. The campaign manager should handle this vital issue with tact in order to avoid causing offence.

2. A visitor should only commence making his or her approaches if fear of rejection can be overcome (i.e. he or she must genuinely believe that prospects listed will respond with gifts). Prospect selection is therefore vitally important.

3. Team members must be encouraged to develop the genuine belief that their work will be an enjoyable experience, not a chore.

4. Where a visitor indicates a personal giving potential lower than that shown on the scale of giving, the campaign manager should speak with the visitor to ensure that he or she understands what is expected.

5. Where a visitor shows constant negativity and avoids making his or her own gift, a graceful way must be found to allow that person to retire from the team with dignity.

As soon as a visitor has made the first call, the campaign manager should call on them, personally and privately, to discuss progress and offer advice as part of a continuing training programme. This is of the greatest importance with members of the major gifts and leadership gifts' committees.

## Visitor kits

During a briefing seminar, visitors should be provided with a kit of information which will reinforce the items discussed during the session and assist them when making their fundraising visits. A visitor kit should contain:
- an explanation of the principles of fundraising
- scale of giving
- organisational structure
- asking for the money leaflet
- details of taxation benefits and taxation tables
- copies of relevant administrative forms (Gift Aid declaration, gift card etc.)
- job descriptions
- campaign progress update
- team progress
- campaign newsletters, copies of recent press clippings etc.
- volunteer updates
- dedicated gifts list
- questions and answers sheet
- campaign brochure.

## Types of fundraising teams

The structure of the fundraising teams will differ from campaign to campaign according to the various constituencies of the organisation. Nevertheless, there are five teams that are usually common to all:
1. **Major gift/leadership:** seeking gifts from affluent individuals or families who have a personal interest in the campaign or who are recognised leaders of the organisation (such as board and staff members).
2. **Corporate:** seeking funds from companies, that may gain marketing, CSR or public relations benefits through their support.
3. **Grants:** seeking grants from trusts, foundations and Government bodies.

4. **Community:** seeking gifts from the remainder of the organisation's constituency.
5. **Bequest/legacy:** encouraging consideration of deferred giving and other planned gifts.

## 1. Major gift/leadership team

It is a feature of Compton campaigns that some of the largest gifts often come from individuals who are not people with high public profiles and ostentatious wealth – they often live quietly, unnoticed. Successful campaigns rely upon the seeking out and involvement of the benefactor.

Visitors will want to ask companies and trusts for money, because there is less personal embarrassment in asking people to give away money which is not their own. To win your capital campaign, begin by seeking out the private benefactor.

Campaign managers will start to promote the search for benefactors early in the campaign so that team members really believe it can be done.

To this end a *Major Gift Prospect Listing Group* should be established which may include:
- influential members of the governing body
- long-serving volunteers or staff
- professionals/business leaders associated with your organisation.

It should be noted that these people may not be the best askers but could be highly effective in identifying prospective benefactors.

Campaign managers will encourage major gift visitors to overcome:
- fear or embarrassment of asking people for their own money
- reluctance to spend the time needed to secure gifts from benefactors
- lack of belief that benefactors can be found and large gifts secured and to:
  - devise strategies for approaching prospective benefactors
  - review personal contacts and decide on the appropriate visitors to make the personal approach

- research the most suitable dedicated gifts to be offered
- decide on the size of the gift being sought.

In seeking benefactors it is vital that we understand the needs of the giver and ensure that we meet them.

It is important to note that the chances for success in achieving the fundraising target will be dramatically increased where the visitors on the major gift/leadership team make their own gifts at this level.

## 2. Corporate team

It is becoming more difficult to attract sizeable corporate gifts. Campaign managers are skilled at developing relationship-marketing packages that provide corporate prospects with the quid pro quo they seek. Working with a team of visitors each of whom has an understanding of, or access to, corporate prospects they should:

- Devise submissions using corporate annual reports detailing co-operative marketing arrangements that provide benefits to prospective corporate givers.
- Develop strategies for lobbying the key decision-makers and stakeholders in an organisation to win support for the submission.
- Formulate who should make the approaches to the organisation, including which part of the organisation should be approached first.
- Create opportunities to provide corporate givers with the desired level of acknowledgement for their support.

## 3. Grants team

Grants from trusts, foundations and other grant-making bodies such as the National Lottery can be achieved for almost every capital fundraising campaign. While the preparation of grant applications is usually a staff-led activity, the solicitation process is best undertaken by influential volunteers working behind the scenes to win support for the formal grant application.

A small team will need to be recruited to oversee all applications for grants. The personal influence of team members will play a key part in securing the size of grant required. The use of 'leverage' in the timing of applications will be a key consideration for the team to address. On occasions, grants will be made to match funds raised from other sources or to challenge the remaining prospects to match the gift being made. The grants team will need to lead this important part of a capital campaign, providing personal insight and possibly even influence with trustees and other 'gate-keepers'.

## 4. Community team

The community team will generally obtain the gifts at the lower end of the scale of giving and approach:

- individuals and family groups
- small businesses
- special interest groups.

The community team will usually have more visitors than other teams, as a larger number of lower level gifts will be required.

The purpose of focusing the structure of the campaign on specific gift categories is to broaden the target area and con-stituency to ensure that the widest possible coverage is achieved.

## 5. Bequest/legacy team

During a capital campaign, many organisations now offer the opportunity for people to declare their legacy gift and settle on how the funds will ultimately be applied – to an endowment or other specific area.

A legacy team will need to be recruited to focus on this specific area of fundraising. Usually made up of other people who have also decided to give a legacy, this team can have an ongoing role beyond the conduct of a specific campaign. (See Chapter 9 for further detail.)

### Specific constituency teams

In some campaigns, rather than form a single community team, it is more appropriate to establish a number of different teams that will cover the various constituencies of the organisation.

Defined 'closed' constituency organisations, such as schools, can if they choose, collect details of every possible prospect who might make a gift, be they parents, past parents, alumni, suppliers, staff or governors. Capital campaigns run by defined constituency organisations often benefit from a team structure that secures gifts at the lower end of the scale of giving, based on year, class or house groups. Effectively, a specific team charged with ensuring that all prospects in their designated area are asked for a gift covers every part of the constituency.

Non-defined 'open' constituency organisations, such as universities, find it difficult to list everyone who may have an interest in them, due to the wide reach of their mission. Anyone with such an interest in the work of the university could technically become a prospect, regardless of whether or not they are or were once enrolled. Nonetheless, it is possible for an open constituency organisation to reach out to its defined audiences.

It is also possible in a capital campaign to establish specific constituency teams that focus on securing gifts for a particular project, such as a library team or a sports pavilion team.

Specific constituency teams can help to focus the efforts of visitors, establishing clear goals and prospect areas to be addressed. Care should be taken, however, to ensure the disciplined management of these teams and guarantee that prospect allocation conflicts are quickly resolved and gifts are secured within the scale of giving.

## Managing fundraising teams

Successful and exciting campaigns are team-based, where each team of visitors is:

- externally focused
- dynamic and interactive
- process-driven
- results-oriented.

The campaign manager is responsible for the efficient management of all the fundraising teams. He or she will organise individual and group meetings with visitors, mindful of the need to be economical with the time taken. Once the teams have been formed, briefed on how to ask for a gift and prospect listed, the management of visitors to ensure the asking is completed becomes critical.

## Progress meetings

It is desirable that at least three progress meetings are held for each fundraising team. The dates and details of these meetings should be announced as far in advance as possible:

- the first will be held a few days after the team starts making visits
- the remainder will be held at appropriate intervals
- at each meeting financial targets should be set for achievement by the next meeting.

A typical format for a progress meeting follows:

1. Campaign chairman or other member of leadership team is present to emphasise the importance of the meeting and to create enthusiasm.

2. Campaign and team totals are announced.

3. Comments and discussion on calls that visitors have made and additional training on fundraising principles.

4. Team leader talks about the importance of the project to the organisation.

5. The meeting should be run in a positive, upbeat manner; should last about one hour and be held at a time that does not detract from visitors making fundraising calls.

The campaign manager is responsible for organising the attendance of visitors at all progress meetings (and any other meetings held during the campaign at which the attendance of visitors is required).

## Visitor targets

An analysis of the scale of giving is an effective strategy to use in convincing visitors and givers that the target is achievable.

The use of individual targets is an equally important strategy in winning campaigns. In meeting with the team, the campaign manager should ask each team member to set a target figure they believe they can achieve from each of their prospects. That target will be the amount they will discuss with the prospective giver as the figure they may consider giving.

The sum of the total of the potential listed for each prospective giver is the visitor's fundraising target. After setting targets for each visitor, the campaign manager will sum up all the visitor targets to ensure that they:

- match the various levels set in the scale of giving
- total more than the campaign target.

Where possible, the total of all the targets should be in the vicinity of double the actual campaign target.

We suggest that the campaign manager does not actually state that the individual targets will total twice the overall target as that will only encourage visitors to believe that if they achieve 50% of each person's target, they will win. This would create unnecessary complacency in the campaign.

## Organisational chart

It is important that all visitors have an overview of the organisation of the campaign in order to understand their specific role. This is best achieved through a briefing on the campaign plan (see Chapter 5), where a detailed team organisational chart is provided.

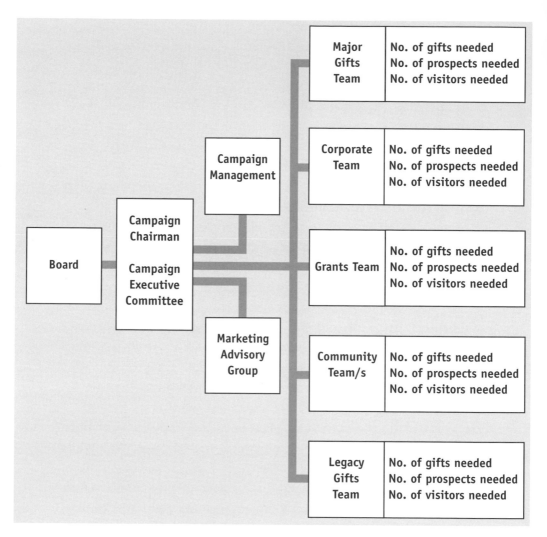

| Major Gifts Team | No. of gifts needed<br>No. of prospects needed<br>No. of visitors needed |
| Corporate Team | No. of gifts needed<br>No. of prospects needed<br>No. of visitors needed |
| Grants Team | No. of gifts needed<br>No. of prospects needed<br>No. of visitors needed |
| Community Team/s | No. of gifts needed<br>No. of prospects needed<br>No. of visitors needed |
| Legacy Gifts Team | No. of gifts needed<br>No. of prospects needed<br>No. of visitors needed |

FIGURE 12: *Organisational chart*

FIG 12

## Campaign office: your visitor nerve centre

The management of the fundraising effort is co-ordinated through the campaign office, located at the heart of the organisation and accessible to visitors and others seeking information.

The campaign office must be busy and businesslike. It should be well equipped with information and communication systems. Well-produced progress charts and boards demonstrating campaign timetables and team lists should heighten the ambience of focus and activity. It is the 'nerve centre' for the campaign and its management is usually trusted to a campaign co-ordinator assigned to ensure that the day-to-day administrative arrangements are in order.

The campaign manager should not be a campaign office fixture, but rather out and about calling on visitors, planning meetings, running training sessions, conducting role plays, accompanying visitors on asking appointments and, generally, feeding the success of the growing number of givers and getters.

## Being the *insistent* voice

Carlton Ketchum, an American pioneer in the art and science of capital fundraising best encapsulated the importance of good campaign management. He explained that at the centre of successful capital fundraising campaigns is the *insistent voice*, the source of suggestion, calling for action, focusing on finding the one sure way to achieve, rather than the thousand plausible reasons for giving it up altogether.

In UK campaigns too, the *insistent voice* is vital to winning major campaigns. Someone simply must be there, calling, prompting, guiding and supporting those who with enthusiasm are giving precious time to the campaign, often busy and over-committed in many other directions.

Someone must know what everyone is doing. Someone must be responsible for getting things done. Someone must understand fundraising methods – be nimble in marshalling key statistics, determining how best to ask who and when, conversant with the distinctions between asking a grant-making body, a company or an individual, from whatever cultural background. Someone must be able to plan inspiring meetings and events, manage publicity, build momentum and excitement and yet never get distracted from what it will take to achieve the target. Someone with an insistent voice must be intimately familiar with the efficient administration of the campaign ensuring that proper systems are established and maintained. There must be someone to organise and train volunteers, and then to create and sustain their enthusiasm.

That someone must be accountable, they must be paid. Experienced, with the judgement and the skill to see the significance of the timing of the campaign … that someone must have the tact to inspire powerful volunteers, the energy and drive to push on through the 'dark night' that comes in every campaign, and the desire, the thirst for victory.

The campaign manager is that voice, seeing that the fundraising runs to plan. Visitors 'do the asking'; they use their access and influence to open doors and secure gifts, but they also have other responsibilities and can only reasonably give part of their time and energy to advance the campaign.

Usually, when the campaign manager leaves things stop happening. Much more could be done; prospects could be followed-up, fresh calls could be made by visitors who are as keen as ever – but they don't.

When we examine the Compton capital campaigns that have achieved their target over the past five decades, one key characteristic is found in all – a strong partnership between volunteer leadership and professional campaign management. Recognising the different contribution to success made by volunteer and professional, we have been fortunate to work with clients who value the *insistent voice* that we bring as campaign managers.

## Summary

- Volunteers are the most powerful askers. They are known as 'visitors'.
- To make the most of volunteer resources, a professional campaign manager is essential to be the 'insistent voice'.
- Visitors will need to be trained how to ask for a gift. They should be equipped with kits of key information and organised into teams.
- The organisational chart for a campaign will show the team structure, which will usually include teams for major gifts/leadership; corporate; grants; community and bequest/legacies.
- Specific constituency teams will be organised differently depending on whether or not the organisation is 'closed' (i.e. school) or 'open' (i.e. university).
- Great campaigns are team-based, where every team of visitors is externally focused, dynamic and interactive, process-driven and results-oriented.

# Chapter 8

# Bringing in the money: the art of asking

Most people believe that asking for a charitable gift is like begging – and it is naturally the last thing they feel comfortable doing at first.

In a recent UK study published in *The Times*, people were quizzed about what they fear doing most; asking for money was at the top of the list, ahead of running down their high street naked or even bungee jumping.

No surprise then that the main reason fundraising campaigns fail is that prospective donors are not asked properly. Rather, when the challenge of raising millions of pounds meets the fear of asking for money, we so often resort to eloquent 'topped and tailed' letters, celebrity events and tin-rattling.

Capital fundraising is a personal business. It is only successful when carefully selected individuals are asked personally by a respected peer to give as generously as they can. Yes, it is possible to do this without becoming a pariah. In fact if done properly, asking for money can boost your standing in the community and win new levels of respect from people across all walks of life.

## Don't just 'cut and paste' American fundraising practice

UK fundraisers can trace much of their current practice back to their American counterparts, but when it comes to talking about money our social and cultural norms are very different. This is important to bear in mind when it comes to successfully applying capital fundraising techniques.

In the UK we cannot simply 'cut and paste' the proven fundraising practices used in the USA and expect them to work as effectively over here.

## Attitudes to money

In the UK we tend to consider it impolite in a social setting to discuss subjects such as politics, religion, sex and money. While some niceties are fading, those related to money remain as strong as ever. Money is the last taboo, and successfully asking for it without losing your friends is a real art.

Even among friends or family, we can be reluctant to discuss our financial affairs in any detail or share information about income or assets. In North America on the other hand, it is not uncommon to be asked in a social context by someone who is not well known to you, 'What do you do for a living?' and even, 'What did you earn last year?' These are questions you rarely, if ever, hear in a British conversation. We tend to judge a person's status through subtler probing, with questions such as, 'So, where do you live?' or, 'What school did you go to?' or even, 'What plans do you have for the weekend?'

Due to the 'average' American's openness about money and direct personal manner, (not to mention major differences in tax regimes) the mechanics of capital fundraising tend to be easier to apply in the USA than in the UK. American fundraising volunteers insist on having a clear understanding about who is making money and who isn't. When it comes to the 'ask', Americans will be more direct about asking for a specific amount.

Ultimately the status game is played differently and this is best demonstrated through the odd phenomenon of published rich lists. While both the USA and UK media produce these league tables of personal wealth, it is interesting that only in the USA do they publish a list of who has given the most to charity. In America, it is the entry of your name on this list that affords greater status, with a commonly held view that you are not truly a millionaire until you have given away your first million.

## Same principles, different application

In managing many of the largest and most challenging capital campaigns in the UK today, we have found it necessary to modify the asking techniques presented in American fundraising texts, while remaining true to underlying principles:

- We started by understanding our different attitudes to asking for money, which does not come naturally to most people who have a basic fear of being rejected by those they know.
- Then we carefully reviewed how best to brief the visitors on the following 'five steps' to help them overcome this fear factor. Taking the time and care to brief visitors will instil greater confidence and help to avoid some of the usual pitfalls associated with asking for a gift.
- Finally, we planned to mentor our visitors, assisting, guiding and debriefing them to ensure that each approach for a gift is given the care and attention it deserves. With success your visitors will grow in confidence and appreciate that they have great power to encourage others to follow their lead.

# Asking: *five steps to success*

Asking for a gift is not an easy process but we are confident that if you apply the following 'five steps', you will not only raise large sums, but you'll also build a network of committed supporters for your organisation.

All volunteer askers, or 'visitors', need to consider each of the following steps when asking for a gift:

## Step 1: Preparing

### Know the story
- Take the time to read through the case statement. Understand why you are raising money and what the benefits will be when the project is completed. Think about which parts of the project will be of greatest interest to your prospects. Try and see the project from their point of view.
- Review the pre-prepared list of questions and answers and marshal any other information that you may need to hand when telling the story.

### Your first gift
- Make your own gift to the campaign at a level on the scale of giving that you believe will encourage others to be as generous as possible. This will demonstrate your commitment to the project and help build an early success factor for the campaign.
- If you can't convince yourself to give, then consider carefully if you are the right person to ask others to do so.

### Your next gift
- List the names of those prospective givers whom you would like to ask. It is important that you have a connection with each prospect and that you are prepared to approach them personally for their gift to the campaign.
- Check with the campaign office to ensure that the people on your list have not already given, or that someone else is about to visit them.

- Put your list in order, starting with the person that you believe is most likely to say yes, rather than the person who is most likely to make the biggest gift.
- Consider carefully where you would like to ask your prospect for his or her gift. Never do so at social occasions, only at pre-arranged appointments when the project can be properly presented. This will avoid embarrassing misunderstandings.
- Decide if you would like someone else to accompany you to visit the prospect. For example, it can be a good idea to invite the executive director, chairman or other institutional leader to be part of an approach to a major gift prospect, or someone else with the knowledge to help you to answer detailed questions.

### Act decisively
- Get your attitude right – remember that you are inviting people you know to join you to support a worthwhile project. You are not asking them to give money to you. Most prospects will be impressed that someone has taken the time and trouble to visit him or her personally.
- Do it now – make asking the prospects on your list a top priority. Help build real momentum for the campaign by getting on with your appointments as soon as possible.

## Step 2: Relating

### Cultivate a 'yes'
- Think about how much each of your prospects knows about the project. Consult with the campaign office to develop a cultivation plan, which might include special events, tours of the project or the use of other communication tools to help build the level of interest your prospect has in the project. Those prospects on your list that are close to your organisation may require very little further cultivation and can be asked quickly.

### Make the appointment
- Personally telephone to make an appointment to visit your prospect. Explain that you would like to call and share with

them the project plans, and will need about half an hour of their undivided attention.

- Do not send the campaign promotional material through the post. If asked to do so, explain that this would not do the project justice; indicate that you would like an appointment to properly explain the benefits of the project and personally answer any questions your prospect may have.
- If appropriate, write or send an email to confirm the arrangements for the appointment. If a fellow volunteer, board member, member of staff, architect or other professional is accompanying you, introduce them in your confirmation letter and explain why you have asked them to attend. No surprises please.
- When asked personally by a peer, there is an 80% chance of a prospect saying yes and making a gift. (They are also significantly more likely to make a bigger gift.)

**Get on the same side**

- At the beginning of your appointment, confirm how much time your prospect has to discuss the project. Then take a few minutes to break the ice (people are usually most at ease when they are talking about themselves). The point is that you need to give everyone time to settle, before getting down to telling the story. However, be careful not to spend too long on the small talk and then rush through the rest of the appointment.
- Mirror your prospect's body language. Subconsciously, people feel more relaxed when talking with others who look and sound like they do. It may seem a little contrived, but if you subtly start adopting a similar pose to your prospect and use some of the same words that they do, you may find that they are generally more receptive to your proposals.
- Over 70% of donors report that it was during the personal appointment that they decided how much to give.

## Step 3: Storytelling

### Tell the story
- Tell the story that inspired you to make a gift to the campaign and talk about those parts of the project that you think might most interest your prospect.
- Address the benefits of the project. Speak of the opportunities that lie ahead if only the funding could be secured. Gone are the days when the 'neediest' charity raised the most money. Today, the language of 'opportunity' motivates major givers.

### Use the promotional material
- Use the promotional material as an outline script to help you tell the story. Highlight items to your prospect, including who else is involved and what pace-setting gifts have already been received. The key to this step is to build confidence and community. Your prospect needs to not only understand what the project is, but who else is backing it – they need to be convinced that the venture has a high probability of success.
- Leaning over the promotional material can allow prospects to relax and focus attention. Always position the brochure to best address the prospect and consider using a pen to point to items of interest and guide the flow of discussion. People's eyes will follow the end of the pen, so be aware of where you are pointing. Usually it is during this stage that the most revealing questions are asked and the genesis of the specific 'ask' is formed.
- The words we actually *say* account for only 7% of our personal communication 'bandwidth', so remember to make the most of your promotional material to help tell the story.

### Investigate questions
- Prospects ask questions, if they are interested. The pre-prepared questions and answer sheet provided by the campaign office will help you to answer most of them, but occasionally there will be something that stumps you. This is fine – just indicate that you will get them the answer and move on.

- One way of determining what your prospect thinks of the project is to ask questions yourself. Try and find out what will motivate your prospect to make a gift and which part of the project holds the greatest interest for them.

## Step 4: Asking

**4**

### Declare your own gift
- Explain why you made your gift and exactly how much you gave. This will help your prospect to decide how much they will give. People do not want to be embarrassed by giving either too little, or too much. Your gift will help set a benchmark they can use to avoid losing face.
- You are not bragging when you declare your own gift, simply providing a helpful way for your prospect to work out what would be the right size of gift for them to make. If you are uncomfortable saying how much you have actually given, consider using your pen to point to a level on the scale of giving when you say, 'I have given at this level to the campaign because …'. Alternatively, you could also indicate that you have given a particular designated gift, which is clearly marked in the promotional material at a certain gift level.
- Whichever route you take, it is absolutely vital that you indicate that you have given and how much. In capital fundraising, it is not the number of gifts that matters, but the size. Your gift will be a powerful influence on the generosity of those you ask.
- Don't be afraid that you are asking for too much. People will not be offended because you think they are wealthier than they are. Often they will be flattered. It is also far easier to reduce the size of gift you are seeking, than it is to increase it. So be bold, think big and set your sights high. More often than not you'll be pleasantly surprised by the generosity of your prospects.
- In your own words, ask: 'When I first became interested in this project, I thought you would be the right person to ask for a gift of £100,000 given your …'. Or even, 'It is ultimately up to people like you and me who believe strongly enough in the work of our organisation, to give £100,000. Will you join me?'

## Offer recognition

- Once you have made a clear ask, *then* move on to address the detail of how the gift would be recognised and the most tax effective ways it could be funded. Do not confuse your prospect with this detail until after you've asked clearly for a specific amount.
- Again, the best way to explain gift recognition opportunities is to talk through how you decided how you would like your gift acknowledged.

## Pledge the gift tax effectively

- Explain, using the scale of giving printed in the campaign promotional material, how your prospect's gift could be pledged for payment over a number of years. This will make even the most 'eye-watering' number look manageable.
- Some prospects will have other financial or charitable commitments, so you may need to encourage them to start their first pledge payment at some point in the future, when their cash flow will allow.
- Gifts to a registered or exempted charity are tax-effective. A moment taken to explain this to your prospect could make a big difference to the amount received. As part of your promotional material, details on the Gift Aid and Gift of Shares schemes should be clearly presented. It is possible that the Inland Revenue could be the biggest single giver to help fund your project, if you present the tax benefits properly.
- Avoid becoming obsessed by these schemes. Government is forever changing them. Simply provide your prospects with the key information and encourage them to seek independent advice if their affairs are complex.

## Listen, then answer questions

- Once you have asked for a gift, stop and listen to what your prospect has to say. You may be surprised.
- People find silence uncomfortable – after a few seconds they will want to fill the void, rather than have it continue. You see, while you've been talking, they have been thinking, and it is

what they are thinking that matters, so now is the time to get
their initial reaction to your request for a gift.

- Usually, your prospect will first respond with a series of
  questions about the project and to clarify exactly what is being
  asked of them. This is the positive response you want.
- Deal with each question, answering as best you can. However,
  do not get distracted. Move forward by revisiting your request
  for a gift, couched in a slightly different way to address their
  question, and then listen again, and so on.

## Step 5: Closing

### Clarify areas of interest

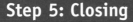

- Eventually, you will be able to clarify your prospect's intentions.
  If they decide to make a gift, take a moment to confirm these
  details using the gift card. Remember that only written
  promises can be counted as pledged gifts to the campaign.
- If after all your efforts the prospect decides not to make a gift,
  rest assured that it will be for very good reasons and simply
  thank them for their time. In every campaign there will be
  prospects who decide not to make a gift. Move on and try not
  to take their decision personally.

### Get the next appointment

- Some prospects will want to consult with others before making
  the final decision about their gift. When this happens, avoid
  leaving things up in the air. Indicate that it is important that you
  know one way or another if they would like to give to the
  campaign. Make clear arrangements to come back and get their
  answer soon.
- Saying 'no' isn't easy, so many prefer to say 'maybe', and then
  do nothing. This is how problems arise – be direct and indicate
  that one way or another it is important for you to know if they
  would like to make a gift. If they say no, then you will be able
  to ensure that no one else asks them. If they say yes, then you'll
  want to get the details straight. Keep it simple and clear. Ambiguity
  at this stage in the process will just cause problems later.

- Pay special attention to the comments people make as they escort you from the room. The business discussion is over, the guard is down and what they are really thinking is often revealed.

## Update
- After the appointment, take a moment to call in to the campaign office and update your campaign manager on the progress made. There may be other helpful snippets of information for you, and an encouraging word or two to assist you with your next prospect.
- Ensure that whatever the outcome of your appointment, within a day write to thank your prospect for the time they have given to consider your request for a gift and to confirm next steps.

## Getting the asking started

The five steps offer a simple but effective way of raising large sums, provided we can encourage volunteers to step beyond their comfort zone and undertake peer-to-peer personal asking. We have found that many will 'intellectualise' the process. They will happily discuss each step in great detail, but remain gripped by a basic fear of losing their friends.

So as professionals, our task is to build confidence and help our volunteer askers to make their first appointment. The tried and tested role play is an excellent place to start. In this 'safe' environment, a valuable opportunity is being provided for your visitors to practise their first 'ask', to examine their preconceptions about asking and learn in a practical way to apply the five steps. Role plays can be especially useful when visitors are asking with others and need to work through how they will conduct the appointment together. They are also useful as a 'dry run' for a particularly important major gift ask to help build confidence and ensure that all eventualities are covered.

## Face up to the fundraising challenge

One of the most successful volunteer fundraising leaders we have ever worked with was known to send post-it notes to fellow board members with the simple, challenging question, 'How many asks have you made today?'

While we are not necessarily advocating that level of zeal, there are no magic wands in fundraising.

Successful fundraising campaigns do not hinge on glossy brochures, list brokerage, name-only patronage, public launches, flashy websites, celebrity endorsements and expensive fundraising events. Dozens of 'appeals' across the UK are failing because of this fallacious approach to fundraising and the fact that there is too little actual asking for the money going on.

There are no short cuts. The money has to be asked for. And, consistently, across all kinds of fundraising programmes, the more personally you ask for a gift – the better the response will be.

A selection of role plays is provided next to help you craft scenarios that will be appropriate to your campaign.  It is important that the role plays are made as realistic as possible, when briefing your visitors.

## Role plays

The key, when conducting role plays is to give each session enough time for the scenario to be played out in real time. Too often these hypothetical situations are conducted in an abridged time frame, which only encourages a similar rushed approach during the real situation.

Remember that our purpose is to build confidence. So once you have highlighted each role play's teaching point, use the rest of the session to encourage your visitors and to build up their courage to undertake this vital role. We have seen some of the most powerful and successful people who on a daily basis face challenging and daunting jobs, approach the prospect of asking for money with genuine reluctance. Never assume that any member of your team will be able to successfully ask for a gift without thorough preparation, careful mentoring and management.

## Role play 1: 'Not enough!'

Your task is to secure the gift of a keen supporter for your organisation. She is enthusiastic, influential and is seen as a key player in the fundraising plan. You know that she has the capacity to pledge a major gift of £10,000, or more, similar to your commitment of £15,000.

When you raise the question of her gift she smiles and enthusiastically hands you a cheque for £1,000 saying that she has put some thought into her gift and wanted it to be meaningful.

*Considerations:*

- How do you raise her sights?
- How do you avoid hurting her feelings?
- How would you guard against this situation arising in the first place?

*Teaching point:*

How to raise the sights of prospects.

*Trainer's checklist:*
- First and foremost thank her for her support.
- Explain why you decided to give £15,000 as a way of explaining the scale of giving and pledging a gift over time.
- Use the designated gift list and other forms of recognition to raise sights.
- Ask if she would be willing to commit to at least the same amount over the five-year giving period.
- Explain how tax benefits (Gift Aid and Gifts of Shares) could also increase the size of the gift.
- Explain how important leadership giving is in raising sights.

## Role play 2: 'Closing the gift'

Throughout the campaign you have been trying to obtain the gift of a prominent local business leader.

You have met with him on several occasions – once over a game of golf, once at a dinner party and once when you bumped into him at a business function. He has always been very friendly, interested, and eager to please.

Whenever conversation has turned to his gift however he answers with phrases such as, 'I'll let you know soon', 'It'll be significant' or 'I'll have to talk to my accountant and I'll let you know'.

*Considerations:*
- How do you get a signed gift card without offending this important person?
- What should be the setting for the meeting?
- How would you avoid this situation arising in the first place?

*Teaching point:*
The necessity of securing a specific appointment for a personal meeting with a prospect in order to close their gift.

*Trainer's checklist:*
- The team member should contact this prospect specifically to secure an appointment to discuss the gift.
- During the appointment, the five steps should be followed.

- If further time is requested, a further appointment must be booked to bring the prospect to the point of decision.
- The prospect may be employing avoidance tactics, and may actually be saying 'no'. By following the face-to-face methodology, you will find out for certain.

## Role play 3: 'Time is money'

As a fundraising team member, you arrange an appointment to meet an old friend and business peer in her offices. You hope to obtain a leadership gift. In the meeting you explain the need, declare your gift and ask for the money. Your prospect however tells you that she strongly believes in the project but has already put considerable time into the organisation and would like to join the fundraising team to show her support.

In short, she does not see why she should have to give money as well – after all her time is valuable as her clients can tell you.

*Considerations:*
- How could you obtain a gift without losing her support in other areas?
- What would be the best possible outcome and how could you best achieve it?

*Teaching point:*
How to demonstrate to this prospect that although her volunteer time is very much appreciated and valued, for the project to proceed money is needed as well.

*Trainer's checklist:*
- Thank them for their involvement in the past – 'I recognise that you give your time freely – I think it is wonderful and I know the organisation is grateful.'
- Tell her that money, in addition to volunteer support, is now required to complete the project, and that although time is valuable, only money will build the new facility/implement the new programme.
- Explain that all members of the fundraising team have

committed their own funds as a show of their leadership to the wider community.

- Indicate that her support on the team would be very much appreciated, and that if she wished, she would be welcome in a team briefing to learn more about the strategy.

## Role play 4: 'Let's all chip in'

You arrange to meet with a prospect who is a vocal member of your organisation and has volunteered his time in the past. You hope to obtain a gift of £10,000.

You talk through the project, declare your own gift, and ask for the money. He replies, 'I don't know what all the fuss is about with this campaign. There are around 1,000 members, so why don't we all give £1,000 and get on with the build?'

*Considerations:*

- How do you explain why asking for an average gift simply will not work?
- How do you raise his sights without offending this important volunteer?

*Teaching point:*

How to explain that asking everyone for an average amount will not work, and why.

*Trainer's checklist:*

- Not everyone will give to the campaign.
- Not everyone will be able to afford the same gift. By the same token, asking those who could afford it or might like to give more or the same as everyone else places a ceiling on the giving.
- Asking for an average gift would be planning to fail.
- We would like to offer opportunities at all levels for people of any means to become 'stakeholders' in this project.

## Role play 5: 'Here we go again'

As a team member who is new to your organisation, you are thoroughly inspired by the campaign and what it plans to achieve. You make an appointment with a friend and seasoned veteran of the organisation to talk about the campaign face-to-face and plan to obtain a significant gift.

Following your presentation, she sighs deeply and replies, 'I know you are new to our organisation, but do you realise they have been talking about doing this for the past ten years? It will never happen, you know. I was on an appeal committee that raised almost £10,000 five years ago ... and nothing ever came of it. People are really sick of hearing about this.'

*Considerations:*

- How would you handle this prospect's scepticism?
- How could you turn the situation around so you obtain a gift and maintain her support?
- What giving options might be best to offer her?
- How could you possibly avoid this situation arising in the first place?

*Teaching point:*

How to handle sceptics and explain why this campaign will be successful when previous fundraising efforts have failed.

*Trainer's checklist:*

- Sympathise with her concerns, but indicate that this campaign has a winning strategy that begins with leadership by example.
- Tell her about the face-to-face asking strategy that is used and the success rates so far.
- Focus on the achievement to date – the amount raised, team members on board, momentum achieved and so on.
- Indicate that she could pledge her support now so it could be counted in the total, but give it later on when building starts/planning permission comes through and so on – OR ask her to give something now, and top it up later.
- Avoid the situation by knowing about the history of the project

in advance and addressing these concerns before they are raised. Alternatively work with another team member on the approach who had the same concerns but has now joined the team and given money.

## Role play 6: 'The great escape'

As an enthusiastic fundraising team member, you arrange an appointment to meet an old friend and business peer in his offices. You hope to obtain a gift of £100,000.

As you meet, he greets you warmly, hands you an envelope and says, 'Good to see you. I know why you're here and, like you, I really believe in the project. Here's my contribution, I hope it helps you out. Would you like a drink?'

*Considerations:*
- Would you open the envelope?
- How do you communicate your expectations?
- How would you avoid this situation arising in the first place?

*Teaching point:*
How to handle this obvious avoidance technique by the prospect to ensure your expectations are communicated?

*Trainer's checklist:*
- Thank the prospect for the gift and early support for the campaign.
- (The danger is that he has not yet seen the scale of giving, and may regret the decision later.)
- Ask if you can open the envelope. This is an essential step in removing the *ambiguity* of the situation. Once you know where things stand, you can address the presentation materials; discuss pledging the gift or even possible designated gifts.
- Ensure that a gift card is also completed, as this is an essential tool in the administration of the campaign.

## Summary

*The art of asking – five steps to success*

### Step 1: Preparing
- know the story
- your first gift
- your next gift
- act decisively.

### Step 2: Relating
- cultivate a 'yes'
- make the appointment
- get on the same side.

### Step 3: Storytelling
- tell the story
- use promotional material
- investigate questions.

### Step 4: Asking
- declare your own gift
- offer recognition
- pledge the gift tax effectively
- listen, then answer questions.

### Step 5: Closing
- clarify areas of interest
- book the next appointment
- update.

# Chapter 9

# Legacies: the ultimate capital gift

## How to build legacies into a capital campaign

Generations of fundraisers have been raised with the 'donor pyramid' (see Chapter 1), which highlights legacies as the ultimate and most valuable form of charitable giving.

In recent years the pyramid graphic has fallen out of favour as an increasingly academic fundraising industry has produced complex legacy-specific research, statistical reports and giving trend projections.

Whatever your preference on how to visualise the importance of legacy giving, the fact remains that a legacy is more often than not the 'final gift from an old friend': the last step on the 'six I' relationship pathway from the prospect's 'identification' and first gift, to what is probably the biggest charitable 'investment' that will be made by the donor.

## The value of legacies to charities in the UK

The facts and figures associated with legacy reporting and trend forecasting can be mind-boggling.

The size and nature of the UK fundraising market has created an understandable fascination with legacy fundraising potential (an ageing population sitting on appreciating property assets).

Legacy analysts in the UK proudly declare that they are at the forefront of demographic research, database segmentation and trend analysis and they produce mountains of data to prove it.

Here are some of the most important headlines:
- CAF's report that £1.07 billion in legacy funding was received by the UK's top 500 charities.
- Seventy-five of these top charities accounted for 80% of that income.
- The total annual market for charitable legacies in the UK is estimated at around £1.5 billion (received from some 90,000 legacies).
- Only around 15% of people who make wills leave something to charity.

**Projected legacy trends over the next 20 years**

Over the next 20 years we will see a massive exchange of wealth from one generation to another, with not just the privileged few with money and assets to leave to family, friends and charities.

The dramatic increase in house prices in the UK created significant adjustments to personal wealth throughout the 1990s, with second generations inheriting properties in addition to owning their own.

For example, one study by merchant bankers Morgan Grenfell reported that the value of inherited property alone quadrupled to £8.5 billion a year in the 1990s. Longer term forecasts project that this will rise even more dramatically over the next two decades, as 21 million people (86% of them pensioners) will become home owners. The predicted inheritance windfalls from property are projected to hit a staggering £35 billion a year by 2025.

**When I get older ...**

Within this statistical melange is the reality that by 2025, some 20% of Britons will be over the age of 65.

And, while healthier living and medical advances will tend to keep more of us alive for longer, the number of prospective legators is still set to dramatically increase.

Indeed, when our generation of fundraisers (now '40-somethings') started our fundraising careers, we were sagely informed that charities could expect to wait from 7–10 years between establishing a legacy programme and seeing the first legacies realised.

Today, we are told by the grim number crunchers that a charity can expect its first actual financial commitments within 3–5 years of establishing a legacy programme. Three to five years: the standard pledge period of most capital fundraising campaigns.

## The 'typical legator'

Furthermore, the specialist researchers can tell us whom we need to be targeting, as years of trawling probate registries in the UK and collating the results of big charity questionnaires has allowed them to build up the profile of a 'typical legator'.

As outlined in *Legacy Fundraising* (a very useful publication sponsored by the Institute of Fundraising, Charities Aid Foundation and Directory of Social Change), the typical legator has the following characteristics:

- She (two-thirds of charitable legators are women) dies in her early 80s and tends to have made her will – or amended it – within a few years of her death.
- She lives alone, as her spouse or partner will have pre-deceased her by several years.
- She is asset rich, but cash poor: probably living on a fixed income, but with her home as the prime asset.
- Her estate will be in the vicinity of £180,000 and she remembers three different charitable organisations in her will (the most popular causes being health care, animal welfare and physical disablement).
- As with 40% of other charitable will-makers, she will have named her solicitor as the executor of her will, and probably hasn't told her selected charities about her legacy.

### Excellent, quantitative facts and statistics ... great for the mass appeal

The time, effort and investment that have been put into legacy research in the UK are highly laudable. It is ideal for those fundraising professionals with a mass appeal cause to market and who find themselves in debate with sceptical trustees about the short, mid and long-term value of legacies.

### Understanding the value ... Pareto principle again

However, one key statistic about the value of legacies is often overlooked and is pretty crucial for the capital fundraiser.
In most analyses of legacy income it is shown that around 20% of legacies represent 80% of the value of all legacies made.

The important Pareto principle (80/20 rule) appears again, and informs us that a relatively few number of legators have the biggest impact.

### Building legacy programmes into capital campaign plans: it's quality fundraising, so use qualitative fundraising principles and techniques

Capital fundraising campaigns should be positioned as extraordinary fundraising efforts at special times in the life and work of not-for-profit organisations.

It is reasonable, in this context, to ask your core supporters to consider extraordinary giving and volunteer work for your cause.

And, if you've been behind the game on legacy promotion, it's a very good time to get your organisation and its supporters up to speed on the subject.

### Legacies: a second string to the volunteer asker's bow

Ideally, all of your face-to-face volunteer fundraisers should be armed with the capacity and confidence not just to ask for cash and cash pledge gifts – but for legacy commitments too.

How often have we heard the phrase:

*'Yes, I'd like to support you with a special major gift, but I haven't got the kind of cash you're after.'*

A strong, person-to-person legacy request (based on a deferred, asset-based gift) provides a very powerful second string to the asker's bow. It allows prospects, who could not otherwise afford it, to make more significant pledges to a campaign.

### Remember who you're asking: the 'donor pyramid' is spot on: legacy fundraising is not 'cold call', factory fundraising

Remember who you are asking for support in capital campaigns: generally, your most loyal and nostalgic supporters – as well as those who are 'cultivated' by those closest to your organisation.

In the capital campaign setting, you can pretty much forget about the fundraising industry's obsession with broader trends, demographics and volume-based percentage games. Remember the common sense of the most valued, core prospects on the 'donor pyramid', because this is largely what you'll be dealing with.

### Beware the 'default' legacy programme

We've seen it dozens of times. It's a shameful waste of volunteer time and charity resources. The policy decision is made – 'we must do more about legacies'. Committees and working groups are formed. Specialist agencies are brought in and make re-hashed presentations on legacy trends – usually with only cursory lip service to any tailored work for the particular organisation. This often leads to an away day on the subject.

A legacy brochure or leaflet is produced (usually with a truly awful pun on the word 'will' in its strapline) and thousands of these mediocre pieces are mass-mailed to databases in the hope that a percentage of 1% will respond.

A usually inexperienced fundraising 'staffer' is put on stand-by and warned about 'not over-stepping the mark' with respondents and then scared half to death themselves with scenarios of how to be ethical, safe, professional and caring when talking to prospective supporters about death and legacies. It's hardly surprising that the majority of UK charities are bewailing a lack of endowment funds.

To quote one ex-board member of a well-known, London-based charitable institution:

*'It reached the point where there was nothing we didn't know about our potential to bring in legacies. We spent endless meetings being told about research, demographics and how our organisation was well placed to become a major beneficiary of legacy income. We spent thousands of pounds designing, producing and mailing out brochures. We're still waiting for the legacies to come in. But, most depressingly, having been asked by the organisation's Director of Development to lead by example – and having agreed to do so – I was never followed up. I'm still waiting to be asked to make my legacy commitment. I'm still, remarkably, willing to do so.'*

### A real, person-to-person legacy fundraising programme

The key to success in legacy fundraising (and capital campaigns give you an ideal opportunity to try it out) is to use person-to-person prospect nomination, cultivation and asking techniques.

### Leadership first ...

Starting with your governing body, and those closest to you, reinforce the importance of leadership, self-help giving – and highlight how legacies can form part of a major gift commitment.

### The six Is – again (applied to legacy fundraising)

At the risk of being pedantic, we're going to trace the legacy fundraising critical path through the 'six Is' again:

**1  Identify**      Those closest to your organisation who should be asked to consider making provisions in their wills (including, importantly, your governing body).

Legator motivation (see 'donor motivation', Chapter 2) will extend to much more than the often-quoted combination of desire for 'immortality and deductibility'.

**Form an identification/legacy prospect review team**
(who firstly agree to make their own legacy commitments) to review your database (and their own networks) and identify like-minded supporters whom they would be prepared to personally approach to also make a legacy commitment.

**Augment this core process with broader prospect identification techniques**
If your organisation has a big database of past givers and supporters, this is the time to enhance the core prospect review process with some soft survey work to encourage legacy prospects (and previously unknown donors) to identify themselves. For example, a number of the UK's hospices have used the survey technique in recent years with very good results.

| | | |
|---|---|---|
| ② | **Inform** | **Plan and host personalised information/ cultivation events**<br>Get your 'champions' to host information events for their invited prospects at your place of operations, board rooms or private homes. |
| ❸ | **Interest** | Focus on the 'emotive' part of the information first – then review practical aspects of making a legacy commitment (including illustrations of possible reduction of inheritance tax liability). The testimonial support of your volunteer leaders who have already made provisions to support your cause in their wills is by far the most persuasive tool at your disposal. |
| | **Input** | As with any other kind of fundraising information event – help attendees to feel that they are having their say and can actually make a difference. The |

bulk of this work is probably done following the information event on a one-to-one basis, with the volunteer champion personally following up the prospective giver.

**⑤ Involvement**  **Present a strong 'recognition club', living legator opportunity**
The majority of legators will like the idea of having their commitment and generosity celebrated while they are still around to enjoy it. So, form an appropriate recognition club (special 'Order', 'President's Circle', 'Patron's Court' or other such device) and offer an annual event to which these VIP givers can be acknowledged and recognised.

Build upbeat legacy theme and promotional materials around people, people benefits and testimonial support – and spend some money on the legacy brochure to differentiate it and make it more substantial and attractive than your run of the mill leaflets.

**⑥ Investment**  **Legacies need to be asked for**
Finally, orchestrate the personal, volunteer-led, peer-to-peer ask.
*'I have made my legacy commitment – will you join me by supporting our special campaign/cause in this way?'*

**Yes – you can and must ask how much**
In the volunteer-led approach, you can suspend much of the apprehension, talk of 'gentle-nudging' and get down to business. Yes, even down to dealing with tabooed questions of 'what kind of legacy?' and 'how much?'

In Compton-managed campaigns, because volunteer fundraisers lead approaches in a peer-to-peer context, our clients can expect to receive written notification that provisions have been made, whether the commitment is pecuniary or residuary, restricted or unrestricted and how much it might, in due course, be worth.

These are down-to-earth, practical matters which long experience suggests prospects have very few hang-ups discussing and which can be openly addressed by well-briefed volunteers. Information on legacy intentions and potential can be vital to your organisation's knowledge of what future capital resources it could have at its disposal.

## Do you have the 'will'?

In almost 50 years of fundraising campaigning, our firm hasn't had one complaint from a prospect about a volunteer-led approach for a legacy.

Many millions have been raised from legacies for our clients, using person-to-person asking techniques which are only slightly varied from those used in classic major gift person-to-person approaches.

Yes, of course, we pride ourselves on helping our clients to choose the best volunteers for this particular fundraising assignment – and the quality of the training and volunteer support given to these champions by our team of campaign managers.

But, we also suspect that there are too many not-for-profits making a meal of it, getting bogged down in research, statistics, scenario planning and codes of practice and not using the power of volunteer askers to achieve legacy fundraising potential.

## As sure as 'death and taxes'

We live in an uncertain world.

CAF's *Charity Trends* report (the definitive annual income survey of major UK charities) outlines a number of factors that could threaten charitable giving from individuals in the UK including:

- mounting personal debt
- increasing commitments to private pensions, health and education
- the impact and cost of global instability, and
- competition for other needs such as to pay for better environmental quality.

However, death is more certain than any of these factors – and none of the above will bother us when we're dead.

## Carpe diem
Over the next 20 years there is going to be a massive inter-generational transfer of asset-based, capital wealth. The continued, rapid rise of property values should increase people's understanding of the need to make a will. UK charities have tremendous opportunities in legacy fundraising. Not just to become more proactive and structured in their legacy campaigns and to use legacies as useful fundraising instruments in project-driven capital campaigns but, literally, to secure the financial stability of their work by using legacies to build significant endowment funds.

## Summary

- A legacy is the ultimate capital gift.
- Over the next 20 years the UK will witness a massive exchange of wealth from one generation to another.
- 20% of legacies left to charity provide 80% of the value of all legacies made to charities in the UK.
- Building legacy programmes into capital campaigns gives volunteer fundraisers an opportunity to get support from cash-limited but asset-rich prospects.
- The most effective way of asking for legacy support is volunteer-led, peer-to-peer asking.
- Be structured and proactive in legacy fundraising – and keep it personal – the long-term financial security of your charity could depend on it.

# Chapter 10

# Information management: recording and reporting

The effective management of a capital fundraising campaign requires the efficient processing of information. It is essential for the campaign manager to know at any given time, exactly how much money has been raised, who is being asked and for how much. Focus on the fundraising effort can only come, when the right things are being measured and reported upon. In so doing busy volunteers will know exactly what they need to do between meetings, not just at the meeting itself.

## Fundraising software

While most capital campaigns are won from 100–150 carefully prepared personal approaches, many hundreds of other, grass roots prospects and givers can play their proportionate roles in funding projects.

A specialist, fundraising database is a vital tool for campaign planning and management. Remember though, that's all a database is – a tool. Good fundraisers understand that fundraising is about people – not endless hours sitting in front of a computer screen.

### Selecting a system that fits your fundraising needs

If you haven't got a fundraising computer system, or are unhappy with the one you are using, think about your big picture needs before getting bogged down in detailed specifications. You probably need a system that:

- uses plain English (rather than codes and computer jargon)
- is accessible by more than one person in your organisation
- focuses on the relationship and involvements you have with your stakeholders (be they givers, members, friends or supporters)
- allows you to adapt 'record cards' to your needs to nominate, list, classify, evaluate and allocate prospects
- links prospect evaluations to the levels of giving you need to achieve (represented by your scale of giving)
- allows you to select and sort groups of records with ease
- offers flexible reporting options (linked to your fundraiser's performance and accountability)
- generates letters and receipts to givers through commonly used word processing packages
- is Inland Revenue approved for automatic calculations and official reports for tax reclaims on Gift Aid giving
- can handle all of your future fundraising activities and campaigns: from membership acquisition to legacies
- is competitively priced, with technical support and training personally delivered at reasonable rates from a UK-based head office.

Finally, you might want to find a fundraising database that has been designed by fundraisers.

Whichever database you use, it is important that campaign staff quickly gain proficiency in the management of the campaign office, which specifically involves the accessing of information, processing of reports and maintenance of accurate financial records.

## Recording of prospects and gifts

The recording of prospects and the details of their gifts is an important part of the administration of the campaign.

Fundamental principles to follow when implementing the recording system are:

1. A computer-generated record card will be established for each prospective giver as soon as possible after they have been listed.
2. The computer will number record cards automatically.
3. The record card should contain as much information as possible about the prospect, including involvements and interests with your organisation, as well as wealth factors and other relevant details that will help in prospect evaluation.
4. The prospect listing cards completed for prospects during prospect listing sessions will be numbered in accordance with the record card.
5. Potential will be recorded on the computer record card upon completion of the prospect listing process. (This potential will be shown in the weekly report.)
6. Gifts will only be entered onto the computer on receipt of a signed gift card or 'letter of intent'. A verbal promise will not be counted until it is confirmed in writing.
7. Dedicated gifts will be entered on the giver's record card when notification is received.
8. All gifts will be manually recorded from the first day of the campaign, on a process sheet, which will enable a check to be maintained on computer entries and automatically generated reports.
9. Throughout the campaign, allocation summaries can be used as a control mechanism to determine the status of the approaches made by each visitor.
10. The campaign manager must know at all times exactly how much has been raised. Failure to know this indicates a lack of management and control.

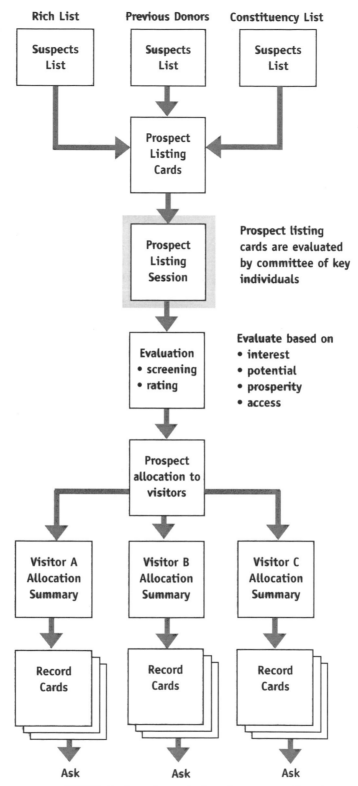

FIGURE 13: *Recording and allocating prospects flow chart*

**FIG 13**

**Prospect listing**

Prospect listing is undertaken by first reviewing lists of suspects, then allocating them to visitors (see Chapter 4).

When conducting a prospect listing session, the campaign manager will prepare prospect-listing cards for consideration at the meeting (see Figure 14 overleaf). Remember that one prospect may in fact be listed by a number of those attending the session, so could have multiple cards. The purpose of the meeting is to decide how best to manage the allocation of that prospect and to agree which visitor should be tasked to ask for a gift.

Also, any one individual may in fact require a number of cards to be prepared because not only could they be a potential giver in his or her own right, but they may also be a trustee of a grant-making body, or even chief executive of a possible corporate donor – in each case a separate card will be needed. It is possible that a different visitor could be allocated to make each of these approaches.

(CAMPAIGN)
## PROSPECT NOMINATION
CONFIDENTIAL

PREPARED BY:

PROSPECT NAME:

THE NOMINEE IS A:

☐ COMPANY *(CONTACT NAME:* )

☐ INDIVIDUAL _____

☐ TRUST *(CONTACT NAME:* )

THE NATURE OF MY ASSOCIATION WITH THE NOMINEE IS:

DO YOU KNOW OF OTHER GIFTS WHICH THE NOMINEE HAS MADE?

HAS THE NOMINEE HAD ANY ASSOCIATION WITH (CAMPAIGN/CLIENT) OR WITH (CAUSE) IN GENERAL?

FIGURE 14: *Sample prospect listing card*

**FIG 14**

### Record card

Once it has been decided which visitor will approach which prospect for a gift, record cards can then be pre-prepared. Record cards provide a means by which gifts can be recorded and the asking process managed – each card is an essential tool in conducting the day-to-day running of the campaign.

The record cards for the prospects allocated to a visitor are partly completed with any known information, such as name, address and so on. The campaign office then issues the cards to the visitor ahead of them making their calls to ask the particular prospect for a gift. It is usual to also issue at the same time the exact quantity of campaign promotional material required to cover the number of listed prospects. Once the visit has been made, the visitor then notes the prospect's response, including details of gift arrangements, on the record card and returns it to the campaign office.

Again, to enable the smooth management of this process, take care to ensure that the following simple, but important steps are taken:

- The printed record card takes its number from the computer-generated record card.
- The record card is given to the visitor prior to making his or her calls.
- It is not necessary to insist that a record card be signed if a cheque is attached, or if another form of documentation is received, such as a letter of intent.
- Record cards and other documentation relating to the gift will be filed alphabetically.
- No gift will be processed or counted in the total raised unless a signed record card or other written confirmation is received.

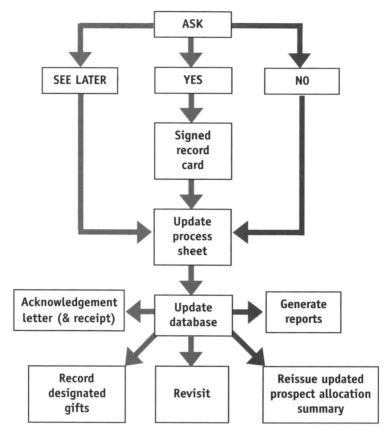

FIGURE 15: *Recording gifts flow chart*

# HBH

## HEART BEAT HOSPITAL

Name: .................................................

Address: ..............................................

.............................................................

...................... Postal Code: .................

Telephone: ...........................................

email:....................................................

Signature: ............................................

Date: ....................................................

I/We would like to designate my/our gift towards the following project/item:

.............................................................

.............................................................

❏ Please send me information on how to make a provision for HBH in my Will.

❏ Data Protection
If you do not wish to receive information from HBH other than that associated with this project please tick here.

Your Pledge:

I/We will contribute a total of : £..................

From ......../......../....... I/We intend to pay:

❏ Monthly ❏ Quarterly ❏ Annually

❏ Other (specify).....................................

Method of payment: (Please check one)
❏ Standing Order (please complete the form below)
❏ Cheque (please make cheque payable to HBH Special Trustees)
❏ Gift of Shares

*gift aid it* *If you are a UK Taxpayer you can increase your donation to us by almost 30% by completing the following Gift Aid Declaration:*

❏ **YES, I would like HBH to reclaim the tax from the Inland Revenue on all donations/ membership subscriptions I make for their work.**

**I understand that I must pay an amount of income tax at least equal to the amount to be reclaimed. I am under no obligation to make any further donation and I can cancel this declaration at any time.**

**(If you are unsure if your gifts qualify for Gift Aid tax relief, please ask your local tax office.)**

### Standing Order Declaration

To The Manager of (your bank) ......................

Address ...................................................

.............................................................

Please pay to:

For the credit of: HBH Special Trustees Account

Sort Code: 00-00-00 Account Number: 12345678

The sum of £.............. on .../..../......
and annually/monthly thereafter on the same date for ...... years OR until further notice.

Name: ....................................................

My account no: ......................................

My bank sort code: .................................

Signature .................................. Date .....................

FIGURE 16: *Sample record card*

**FIG 16**

**Information management: recording and reporting** 147

## Allocation summary

Once the prospect listing sessions have been completed and the record cards pre-prepared, the campaign manager should then prepare in triplicate, an allocation summary for each visitor. These summaries show the status of each approach for a gift being made by each visitor. The summary is usually prepared by the software and is issued ahead of team progress meetings to assist in reporting on the steps being taken to complete the visits.

One copy of the summary is given to the visitor, one copy is kept at the office and a copy is also given to the chairman of the particular campaign team.

| ▆▆▆▆▆▆▆ **Allocation Summary** | | | as at Tue, Oct 1, 2002 |
|---|---|---|---|

**Visit, Mr Will (12)**

**Approaches in progress**

| ID | Name | Date | Status & Comments |
|---|---|---|---|
| 61 | Ralph, Mr John | 28/8/02 | |

**Approaches completed**

| ID | Name | Date | Response |
|---|---|---|---|
| 15 | Davidson, Mr William (Bill) | 2/9/92 | Refusal |
| 9 | Farrow, Mr Roger | 31/8/92 | Gift of £3,896 |
| 12 | Visit, Mr Will | 1/9/92 | Gift of £97,402 |
| 19 | Wjoz, Mr Kim | 1/7/92 | Gift of £2,666 |

**Totals**

**Visitor:** 104,749.03     **Teams:** Foundation Northern Team: 984,029.37     **Campaign:** 5,445,628.57

FIGURE 17: *Sample allocation summary*

**FIG 17**

**Process sheet**

The information management of a campaign will need to have built-in 'checks and balances' to confirm accuracy and provide a sensible back up. We do this by compiling process sheets on which the campaign manager records a summary of the details of all gifts. In so doing it is possible to cross-check campaign totals with those generated by the computer system.

Again, to enable the smooth management of this process take care to ensure that the following simple, but important steps are taken:

- The number of each entry will be noted on the record card, for cross-referencing purposes.
- The process sheet campaign total will be reconciled with the computer-generated figure on a weekly basis.

| DATE | NAME | ENTRY | REC NO | GIFT | | | | | | | RUNNING TOTAL | NOTES | CII |
|------|------|-------|--------|------|------|---------|-----|------|------|-----|---------------|-------|-----|
| | | | | ONCE | GIFT AID | BEQ | GIFT | TAX | | | | | |

FIGURE 18: *Sample process sheet*

**FIG 18**

# Reporting

Regular written reports provide a clear basis for monitoring the progress of the campaign against the goals detailed in the campaign plan (see Chapter 5). Action can then be taken to address areas of concern or progress opportunities that have emerged. Good reporting removes much of the 'hit and miss' experienced in poorly managed campaigns. It instils confidence and keeps key people engaged in the campaign.

Specific reports may need to be developed to address the needs of major funding agencies, such as the Arts Council and National Lottery. Indeed, many trusts and foundations now also require detailed reporting on the progress of the campaign in order to be able to draw down the payment of grants.

## Tips for good reporting

1. Ensure the information collected is accurate.
2. Agree exactly who will get what report and how often (usually as part of the development of your campaign plan).
3. Write all reports in a factual manner, supporting all key observations with statistics.

## Weekly management report

Time passes very quickly when you are capital campaigning. To help ensure what must be done today is in fact completed; a weekly reporting system will need to be implemented.

Every Friday evening, the campaign manager should prepare a weekly management report on the status of the campaign and circulate it to all the members of the Campaign Executive Committee (CEC) for consideration over the weekend. Ideally, the CEC would then meet on the following Monday to consider and agree the priorities for the week ahead.

A good software package will generate a summary of the key campaign statistics, especially progress against the scale of giving, not only in gifts secured but also potential gifts listed from prospects that are soon to be asked. The campaign manager should then add brief comments comprising *no more than five bullet points* for each of the **Achievements** this week and the **Objectives** for next week.

**Monthly progress report**

We usually recommend that a written monthly report be prepared for circulation to the leadership of the campaign and the organisation, providing a concise summary of the state of the fundraising. This report is usually no more than four pages long and must be an honest assessment of the results so far. The report is best presented by the campaign manager in person to a meeting of the Campaign Executive Committee, so that any questions are answered directly.

It is vital that this report accurately presents current problems with the progress of the campaign and clearly details what action needs to be taken to rectify the position.

A monthly report should cover the following headings:

* **campaign status** (progress against the scale of giving)
* **comments on statistics** such as the number of pledges secured and the number of verbal pledges still outstanding
* **team status** (the number of visitors needed; the number enlisted; the number of information events planned and held and their outcome)
* **top 20 prospects breakdown**, with details on the size of potential gifts and the next steps being taken to secure the gift
* **achievements** of the past month and objectives for the next month, as a summary only, against the milestones detailed in the campaign plan
* **recommendations** for action.

**Campaign report**

The campaign report is a detailed account of the history, current status and future potential of the campaign. This report is usually prepared and presented at key moments in the campaign, such as a major review meeting. A campaign report should always be prepared at the end of the campaign to ensure that an accurate record of the fundraising is retained by the organisation and that lessons can be learned for future benefit. We often find that a few years after a major capital campaign has been conducted, little information is retained by the organisation. Key members of staff change, consultants come and go, with vital information on major donors and other valuable insights lost. The campaign report should hopefully ensure that this does not happen (unless the report is also lost).

We usually start preparing the campaign report on the very first day of the management of the campaign. By starting early, key information can be collected, salient points are not missed and by avoiding a last minute rush to complete the report, adequate time is available to review the final draft.

The campaign plan should be referred to throughout the campaign report, which must indicate how the campaign ultimately performed against the projections in the plan.

Statistical and other reports, such as team member prospect listing details are usually obtained directly from the fundraising software.

The report is best arranged under the following headings:

1. Executive summary (major points).
2. Contents.
3. Introduction (findings of the Resources Study etc.).
4. Statistics:
    a. Campaign progress.
    b. Team summaries.
    c. Dedicated gifts.
    d. Cash flow annual summary (based on record card details).
5. Pledge auditor's report. (It is good practice at this stage in the campaign for record cards and process sheets to be verified in writing by an authorised person, who is not involved in the management of the campaign.)
6. The campaign. (History, campaign plan, comparisons, any changes of tactics and why, what still remains to be done.)
7. The structure. (Chart of fundraising team from governing body to number of prospective givers.)
8. The members of the fundraising team. (Team directories, allocation summaries.)
9. Marketing plan. (Press clippings are included in the campaign record book.)
10. Observations and recommendations – an objective assessment

of the status of the campaign with firm recommendations for an ongoing strategy aimed at:

**a.** Reaching target, if this has not already been achieved.

**b.** Continuing fundraising, i.e. annual giving, bequests and so on.

**11.** Ongoing campaign management.

**12.** Campaign expenses budget – summary of status.

**13.** Other relevant information.

**14.** Acknowledgements.

The campaign report is a valuable document. It may make constructive criticism, but it must not contain reference to anyone by name. In any event, whatever criticisms are made must first be discussed with key leaders of the campaign before the report is presented.

Care should also be taken to ensure that the report is smartly presented and properly proofed with a table of contents detailing sections, titles and page numbers. This will hopefully make it easier to use for future reference and prevent the report from being relegated to a dusty shelf.

Once the draft report has been prepared, we usually give a copy to the chairman of the organisation mounting the campaign. We then meet to review the content and decide who should receive final copies and how the report should be presented. The campaign report is packed with highly confidential and valuable information, so great care should be taken when making these decisions.

### Campaign record book

It is useful to prepare a record book detailing all the meeting notes and financial records of the campaign. The record book should also contain a copy of all reports (weekly, monthly and campaign) as well as other key documents and relevant press clippings.

Again, we've found it best to begin the preparation of the record book at the beginning of the campaign. Copies are usually prepared for the campaign chairman, the executive director of the organisation and other key leaders identified at the start of the campaign.

Consider if you want to include electronic copies of promotional material and other key documents with each record book. It may also be sensible to include a 'download' of giving information for the campaign.

The campaign record book often forms part of an overall archiving plan for an organisation, bearing in mind the provisions of the Data Protection Act. Remember that a back up of key financial information will be essential for future reference, but other details may need to be cleared from the computer system. Again, decisions about archiving policy and data retention are best made at the beginning of the campaign, not at the end.

## Summary

- Capital fundraising is a highly measurable activity.
- Effective campaign management is about knowing who is asking who for what, when and for how much.
- A specialist, fundraising database is a vital tool for campaign planning and management, but remember, that's all a database is – a tool. Good fundraisers understand that fundraising is about people – not endless hours sitting in front of a computer screen.
- Regular written reports provide a clear basis for monitoring the progress of the campaign against the goals detailed in the campaign plan. Action can then be taken to address areas of concern or progress opportunities that have emerged.
- Good reporting removes much of the 'hit and miss' experienced in poorly managed campaigns. It instils confidence and keeps key people engaged in the campaign.

# Chapter 11

# Telling the story: campaign communications

## Public relations and communications work in major gift and capital campaigns

Good fundraisers are, first and foremost, good storytellers.

The ability to communicate a core fundraising story to key audiences, as part of a person-to-person approach, is at the heart of most capital and major gift fundraising campaigns.

Some fundraising purists would say that all a well-trained fundraising volunteer needs to ask others for money is their own declaration of what led them to make their own financial commitment – followed by an 'eyeball to eyeball' ask of the like-minded prospect to join them in making a carefully considered gift or pledge.

The reality is that even the most experienced or confident of person-to-person askers will need an aide-memoir or promotional prop to help them with their personal approaches for big gifts.

Exactly which promotional and communications tools are needed will depend on the kind of fundraising campaign you are conducting.

However, the key element in designing fundraising promotional materials is that they should enhance the volunteer and staff fundraising team's ability to 'tell the story' and pave the way for a person-to-person solicitation.

## Everyone's a PR expert and no one wants to fundraise

For every person who tells you that they 'do not know much about fundraising, so don't ask me to ask for money', it is usually possible to find ten people who are public relations experts.

As a board member tasked with the responsibility of making a fundraising campaign work, a volunteer fundraising leader, a director of development or a campaign manager – you will find that everyone wants to edit the campaign brochure, debate the effectiveness of the campaign theme or even redesign the logo. Others will know 'a friend of a friend' in advertising who can guarantee that the cause gets more exposure by helping to win a design award.

Why? Because people are generally uncomfortable with the concept of personal giving and personal asking that is central to the planning, management and success of major gift campaigns. Yet, in comparison, people think that campaign awareness, outreach, community relations, PR, external relations, community relations, media liaison, and, publicity work (or whatever your organisation chooses to call the activity) is *easy*.

## Public relations and publicity

First of all, we need some definitions to cut through the jargon that comes with the communications sector. Keeping it simple (and acknowledging that the many 'experts' out there might disagree with such simplicity):

- Public relations is the creation of a positive environment through the design, creation and distribution of positive messages about your organisation or cause to your key audiences.
- Publicity is one of the ways an organisation or cause can get its message across and, in so doing, create a positive public or community relations environment.

## PR for fundraising

Taking the above definitions further, there are two types of PR for fundraising:

- 'Awareness': a broad-based programme to increase general understanding of an organisation's mission, history, achievements, current work and the benefit of that work to people and communities.
- 'Cultivation': more targeted and personalised briefing of prospective leaders, opinion formers or key audiences to pave the way for their enlistment as fundraising champions or givers.

PR and publicity programmes set the scene for successful fundraising by helping to 'cultivate' fundraising volunteer leaders and increase general 'awareness' of the cause so that their initial calls and visits are well received.

However, PR and publicity alone, generally, do not raise big money. Major gifts have to be solicited in person.

How then is it possible to work through this seductive mass of potentially time-wasting and expensive PR and promotional opportunity to focus us on what is actually needed to pave the way for successful asking and giving?

## The most expensive (and valuable) words in PR consulting

As fundraising consultants we are privileged to work with consultants in other fields and sectors. We have seen our fair share of PR consultants along the way.

Our experience suggests that the most expensive (and valuable) words in PR consulting are: *'Why are you doing this?'*

In fact, these words are so powerful that we often find ourselves using them, and the key question that they form relates to how fundraising managers should or should not use their time. In other words, focus on what *must* be done to get results rather than what might feel nice or, on the face of it, easier to do.

## Where to begin: the fundraising campaign marketing brief

Where we usually start with our clients is to review what the organisation has already been doing to position and promote itself and what in-house PR resources (people, relationships, existing promotional tools and outlets) are available to the campaign.

At an early stage in the planning phase of a campaign, we then draft a framework for PR and publicity action, which we call a 'campaign marketing brief'.

## Four main questions:

The campaign marketing brief is built around four main questions:

1. What message do we want to get across?
2. To which audiences?
3. Through which information, media and communications outlets?
4. With what promotional/communications tools?

### 1. What message do we want to get across? Refining and evolving the case statement.

This is where the early work done on drafting the test case statement and validating it in the resources study is so important.

Take the guidance and input you received in study interviews, refine the case statement and your core 'story' should be ready. Most good stories have a structure: a beginning, middle and end. In summary, a sentence or two applied to each of the following framework points should help to flesh out your formative case statement and ensure that the narrative flows in a way that lends itself to being told by many fundraising volunteers in a consistent way:

### Case statement/'story' framework

- Mission.
- History.
- Achievements.
- Challenges ahead.
- Response to those challenges: the capital project.
- Fundraising goal.
- Benefits of the project to the community.
- Leadership and success to date.
- Opportunities for tax-effective giving.
- Opportunities for giver recognition.
- Vision of the future.
- We need you. Join us, because we have an exciting vision, anchored down by an attractive, urgent and specific project that will make a difference.

The above running order forms the structure for campaign brochures, proposals, core scripts for events and other promotional tools.

Ideally, the fundraising story should be encapsulated in a bullet point summary (one page) and refined into a campaign theme/strapline and logo that literally and visually brands the essence of the campaign.

For examples and 'case studies' of how our clients have refined their case statements through the promotion of campaign themes, straplines and logos, visit the 'Client Spotlights' section of the Compton website at www.ComptonInternational.co.uk

### 2. Who are we trying to reach? Which audiences?

Once again, the resources study leads the way here, because the report and outline campaign plan should have identified the audiences you need to reach to 'tell the story' and ask for money.

Your target audiences will move from the inner core of your 'constituency circle' (for example your governing body and previous financial supporters) to the wider public at large (if, indeed, you have the potential to reach out in a broad-based appeal).

How you design and produce your fundraising promotional materials will need to relate to the ethos of your organisation. For example, if you have a strong, democratic grass roots support base, high production value glossy brochures can be counter-productive. There again, if you are targeting corporate partners, their marketing people will want to see that their brand is being associated with quality, professional promotional pieces.

You might need different materials for different segments of your audience and for different phases of your campaign. As ever, it's horses for courses – but, be sure of whom you're approaching, why and what is needed to get that audience to the point where a fundraising volunteer can ask them for money.

### 3. How do we plan to get the message across – through which outlets?

Once you are sure of your target audiences, you need to work out how best to reach them. At this point, remember to ask 'why are we doing this?' For example, we do not, in the early stages of a capital campaign, need to tell the whole world about it. Initially, we are looking for as much money from as few major givers as possible.

So, how can we inform and interest prospective donors in a targeted way?

### Information events: 'Cultivation', storytelling and volunteer enlistment opportunities

There is one, central cultivation and storytelling opportunity in fundraising campaigning: the 'information event'.

Information events can take many different forms, from breakfast boardroom meetings to more informal gatherings in the homes of prospective volunteers. Often, information events are staged or linked to tours of the project itself, but they all have a similar framework.

| Information event: running order | |
|---|---|
| Host | Welcome and introductions. 'Why I'm involved in this project as a fundraising volunteer.' |
| Institutional leader | The headmaster, chief executive, medical director or other institutional leader. 'Why our project is so important, why we need your help and how you will make a difference.' |
| Q&A | Host chairs questions and answer session. |
| Fundraising manager | The fundraising plan. Person-to-person approaches for major, tax-effective gifts – how to get involved. |
| Host | Thanks attendees and promises personal follow-up as next step. |

Generally, money is not asked for at information events. These gatherings are about teasing out interest of prospective champions and paving the way for individuals and organisations to get involved in the campaign – by making major financial commitments and helping to spread the story through more information events.

### But where are the advertising agencies, newspapers, television programmes, radio stations, websites, gala dinners, concerts and launch parties?

Remember, again, 'why are we doing this?' In the early stages of a major gift campaign we want to cultivate and ask people of influence, power and wealth to give and get money.

Experience tells us that roughly 80% of our goal will come from 20% of the givers. If possible, we need to break the back of the campaign by reaching that key 20% with the big money.

We won't do that through mass media 'awareness' outlets. We will do it through 'cultivation' techniques. And, in capital campaigns, that means dozens of information events – from the beginning of the campaign, right through until the end.

Other events have their place in major gift campaigns: perhaps, as public launches and thank you parties for volunteer workers. So, if your organisation already has key dates in the diary for concerts, gala events and other gatherings, consider how they (or at least some part of these ready-made assemblies of stakeholders and prospects) can be brought into the campaign information event strategy.

Before the money is asked for and starts coming in, major gift campaigns can be measured by the number of quality information events planned and delivered.

### 4. What resources do we need to reach our audiences? Promotional and communications tools.

By now, you'll probably appreciate where we're coming from on the campaign communications issue.

If you are planning and managing a capital or major gifts campaign with an initial focus on getting as much money as possible from as few prospects as possible, you will not need thousands of brochures and extravagant publicity plans.

---

**The major gift fundraiser's promotional plan**

In the spirit of pure capital fundraising, we suggest that most major gift campaigns could be delivered with the following promotional tools:

- A quality campaign brochure (based on the case statement) that can be used as a person-to-person visiting tool rather than a mailing piece (with giving opportunity, tax-effective giving and question and answer inserts).
- A quality, PowerPoint presentation (for use in information events and approaches).
- A broader, grass roots leaflet (or summary of the main brochure).
- Depending on your audience, a stand-alone legacy brochure.
- A concise, core written proposal – based on information from the case statement.
- Gift and pledge forms.

---

It can be, and probably should be, as simple as that.

You might want to form a 'marketing advisory group' to help you design and produce these promotional materials. (This might be two or three volunteers known to your organisation from the world of advertising, PR, design and production.)

On short capital campaigns, managers would have their brochures produced within the first two weeks and half the goal pledged by the time of a public launch event (to thank volunteers and givers and inspire prospective supporters to join them in a successful project).

Following the launch, there might be a few weeks of concerted effort to get press/media coverage of the growing fundraising success and momentum. Depending on the nature of the audience, there might well be a phased, bolt-on grass roots appeal (hopefully more imaginative than 'buy a brick'). The timing of grass roots appeals linked to capital campaigns can vary widely from organisation to organisation.

There would certainly be regular, double-sided A4 campaign bulletins from campaign office to the growing 'family' of givers and workers.

Apart from that, dozens of information events and follow up 'asks' in between, the only other major event in the life of the campaign would be the 'victory party' at the end.

## A fundraising communications tools checklist

It is more cost-effective and productive to keep things simple by challenging yourself and your campaign team to emulate the 'purist's' promotional plan.

But every organisation and campaign is different, and the following fundraising communications tools checklist covers most of the promotional devices we've seen employed over the last five decades of fundraising campaigning and grass roots appeals.

| | |
|---|---|
| *annual report* | How does it represent you to a potential donor? Does it talk about and offer ways of giving? |
| *audio visual* | DVD presentations (and hard copy materials derived from them) used at information meetings, information events and campaign launches/briefings. |
| *broadsheet* | Can be of great use with broader-based awareness programmes and grass roots appeals. |
| *brochure* | Full production piece based on the case statement. A person-to-person asking tool rather than a mailing piece. The campaign's primary promotional piece. |
| *bulletins* | With campaign theme and logo to growing list of donors, sponsors and fundraising volunteers to share good news, recognise volunteer performance and maintain momentum. |
| *business/ strategic plan* | Will be needed for bigger donors and trusts. Your case statement should feed into it. You cannot divorce fundraising from institutional planning. |
| | |

| | |
|---|---|
| *case statement* | Factual, comprehensive and concise document summarising why the organisation needs and merits financial support and offering specific details of the campaign. The **Case for Support** is a more detailed version used as a definitive resource document throughout the campaign. |
| *celebrity support* | Who's on your list? Pre-approved photos and testimonial quotes? |
| *database* | Forget the trials and tribulations – get one that works for segmented communications and fundraising campaigning, is user-friendly, reasonably priced and well supported. |
| *direct mail programmes* | Who's scheduling, designing, writing and responsible for distribution? Annual programme of at least 3–4 mailings. 'Mail and dial' campaigns are traditionally used to 'mop up' prospects in capital campaigns. |
| *Direct Response Television (DRTV)* | The capital campaigner's worst nightmare. The jury's still out on the effectiveness of these programmes in the UK. |
| *donor recognition* | Certificates (and more up-market pieces) that might be used to recognise volunteers. |
| *email* | Great for volunteer updates and e-bulletin delivery. |
| *employee leaflet* | In-house fundraising leaflet offering 'give as you earn' and other 'self-help' initiatives. |
| *envelope stock* | What do your envelopes say about you? (However, if possible, try to avoid the three-hour envelope design session.) |

| events packs | Special packs for runners, swimmers, schools, 'challenge events' and so on including sponsor forms. |
|---|---|
| *fundraising ideas* | 'A–Z' of what supporters can do to raise money (hopefully with an emphasis on the value of actually asking for it). |
| *gift/pledge form* | Special forms on which donors and sponsors can confirm the details of their gift or pledge. |
| *giving opportunity list* | A sight-raising piece, based on the financial need expressed in the scale of giving; highlighting what donors and sponsors can get for their money. |
| *grass roots leaflet* | Simplified, A5 version of the main campaign leaflet brochure with 'how you can help' section. Volume piece for public phase of the campaign. |
| *group fundraising* | 'How to set up a support group' and fundraising ideas. |
| *handwritten notes* | Thank you notes from campaign and institutional leaders to volunteer fundraisers. |
| *legacy brochure* | Legacy campaigns usually warrant a dedicated, stand-alone brochure or leaflet. |
| *letterhead* | Campaign livery: letterhead, compliment slips, business cards and other 'collateral'. |
| *logo* | Differentiate particular fundraising campaigns with this visual interpretation of the campaign's theme. A readily identifiable campaign symbol that encapsulates the project on all campaign materials. |

| | |
|---|---|
| *media adoption* | Every fundraiser's dream, and often feasible if properly managed. Regular, structured stories with newspaper readership response opportunities. Can be very effective if synchronised with the public phase launch of a capital campaign. |
| *media kit* | Packet of materials distributed at press briefing/launch. Should include several articles from which a single comprehensive major story can be written or which may be used individually (e.g. general story on building programme, campaign launch, biographies of volunteer/ celebrity leaders, patient stories and R&D innovations). Should include approved quotes, artwork and photo stock. |
| *media launch* | If you've got a campaign that can benefit from getting the press and media together in one session. |
| *in-house newsletter* | We see some very tired, formulaic and poorly designed charity newsletters. If you are putting a newsletter piece out on a regular basis, use the capital campaign to freshen it up. |
| *in-house newspaper* | As above, if you have an in-house newspaper, make the most of it. |
| *outdoor adverts* | Can be an especially useful awareness or public launch tool if located along heavily travelled roadways and intersections. Most useful for a campaign that has reached a 'public appeal' stage. |
| *photo stock* | It's true. A picture is worth a thousand words. Many a brochure's been spoiled for the want of good photographs. Don't skimp here. It's a false |

| | |
|---|---|
| | economy. Bring in a professional photographer to help your organisation build up its photo library. And keep it fresh. |
| *posters* | Awareness, information and call to action. |
| *PowerPoint presentations* | Stand-alone or linked to CD-ROM presentations. Very useful for information events and, in hard copy form, an adaptable, attractive alternative to a traditional funding brochure or proposal. |
| *promotional goods* | Badges, balloons, T-shirts, bumper stickers and other paraphernalia. |
| *proposals* | Carefully prepared and customised written proposals to individuals, corporations, foundations and other prospective supporters. Ideally delivered following a personal visit (to find out what needs to be in them to ensure success). |
| *public launch* | Some form of major event to note the launch of the public phase of the capital campaign. Ideally, at the stage of a campaign where 50% or more of the goal has been reached so that givers and volunteer workers can be thanked and prospective givers inspired to join them in the days and weeks following the launch. The general message *'We're successful – and making a difference through a special project. Join us.'* |
| *question and answers piece* | Frequently Asked Questions (FAQs) piece which anticipates and inoculates against prospect questions. |
| *signage* | Site signage and street banners. In copy terms, less is more. |

| | |
|---|---|
| *speakers' panel* | Do you have half a dozen institutional leaders who will all follow the script and inject vision and passion into 'stump' speeches and addresses? |
| *sponsor forms* | For events and community fundraising galore |
| *thank you letters* | So important – and so often neglected. |
| *volunteer pack* | Confirms job description, plan, organisation, timetable, training guides and prospect allocations. |
| *ways of giving* | Cash gifts, 'pledges', shares, legacies, gifts-in-kind, gifts of property and assets. You cannot run an effective fundraising campaign without knowing and talking about tax-effective ways of giving. |
| *website* | 'How to give'. Banner campaigns? Online donations? At least, an attractive, animated presentation of your fundraising 'story'. |

View this checklist as a 'menu' of which communications tools are available to your fundraising campaign – but, as with all menus, there is a price on all of the items. So make sure there is a good practical reason behind your choice and that you can afford the items you select.

### Conclusion: personal approaches to targeted audiences

We live in an ever more complicated world with escalating opportunities to get our stories across through exciting and evolving media outlets.

Capital and major gift fundraising campaigns are about setting the scene for, and delivering personal approaches to, targeted sources of prospective high level support.

Your capital campaign communications plan should be based on reaching these key people. So don't be seduced by the latest fads and trends from the PR and communications sector or be trapped by what appears to be the easy option. And, if you want a communications programme that paves the way for successful and cost-effective major gifts fundraising, constantly ask yourself: 'Why are we doing this?'

## Summary

- Communications work for capital fundraising should be geared to 'telling the story' and paving the way for volunteer champion enlistment and asking.
- Publicity alone does not raise big money.
- PR and communications work can be seductive, expensive and potentially time-consuming.
- Draw up a campaign marketing brief to answer four key questions:
    1. What message do we want to get across?
    2. To which audience?
    3. Through which information, media and communications outlets?
    4. With what promotional/communications tools?

The main storytelling, 'cultivation' and volunteer enlistment outlet in capital and major gift campaigns is the targeted 'information event' rather than the mass media 'awareness' channels. Keep it simple: most of the communications and promotional tools needed for a capital campaign are drawn from the refined case statement.
These core fundraising tools can be augmented by items from the 'communications checklist' – but do not lose your focus and choose wisely, because all of them have a price.

Constantly ask, *'Why are we doing this?'*

# Chapter 12

# The Compton Way: making it work for you

## Not a science, but an art

While we employ the logic of scales of giving and the mechanics of prospect identification, evaluation and allocation to manage our campaigns, the use of these fundraising tools does not make capital fundraising a science. Yet many hanker for fundraising to be precise to quantify the results and easily predict the outcomes. This is understandable, given the risks taken by an organisation when mounting a major capital fundraising campaign.

However, the wise trustee is not fooled by the terminology of the blustering expert. He or she knows that success in this arena depends on mastering the art of applying the fundraising tools. Trustees experienced in this field recognise that to raise large sums of money in a relatively short space of time, creativity must triumph over 'cut and paste' solutions. They understand that success comes from a combination of essential ingredients, rarely repeated in precise measure from one campaign to another (even for the same organisation), but always present in every successful capital fundraising campaign:

- **leadership by example**
- **professional campaign management.**

The experienced trustee knows that volunteers are the most powerful fundraisers. When mounting a capital fundraising campaign, they know that volunteer askers are the key resource to win, because with them will come the money, real contacts, genuine influence and the drive for the campaign to succeed.

## Leadership by example

To win your capital fundraising campaign, as chairman you cannot simply be the administrator – sit back and push paper around or conduct 'masterful' meetings. Successful capital campaigns do not hinge on extensive painstaking research, the building of a perfectly segmented database, or award-winning promotional material. This particular type of fundraising is about putting money into a bank account as quickly and as painlessly as possible. To do that you need to actively participate as a leader in the fundraising team.

The accomplished fundraising chairman will engage his team, sharing what's on his mind, yet always remaining confident about the direction of the campaign. These leaders are prepared to argue constructively with team members about the principles of capital fundraising. Indeed, on occasions we have seen highly effective chairmen actively seek out such debate, in the full knowledge that to do so will convert those who may otherwise privately disagree with the principles, but not be prepared to speak up. Active leadership will counter the inertia created by naysayers and is vital if common sense fundraising principles are to prevail.

### You can't do it all

Many people think that they are the only ones who can do a job properly. For some reason, one of the hardest things in the world seems to be letting someone else get on with a task that is really important to us. Yet to win a fundraising campaign, it is absolutely essential that this happens.

Except in the most rare of circumstances, human beings do not operate well in splendid isolation – even the solo round-the-world sailor has to rely on a team to undertake the necessary preparations and essential back up. While they must confront the challenge before them, the sailor does so in full knowledge of the team of friends, family and colleagues who are 'working with them' throughout their ordeal.

Likewise many a performer in sport or the arts will agree that their game or show significantly improves when they are before an audience. Why? Because we do not want to be embarrassed, it matters to us what other people think and very often we do not want to let the team down.

The same dynamics are present in a fundraising campaign. In our experience people work best as part of a team. Through the interaction of egos and personalities the business of managing a vibrant fundraising team can at times be frustrating and demanding. However, this often powerful exchange is the chemistry of success, because only then will the team be developing the momentum and confidence necessary to achieve the target.

It amazes us how frequently we encounter the view that just one or two people can raise a sizeable sum (usually it is suggested, members of staff). Even campaigns that endeavour to secure only major gifts still need a team of five or more volunteer visitors.

Team enlistment is one of the most basic essentials of a successful capital campaign. As campaign managers, we have found that probably the hardest job of all is to enlist the fundraising team. When training new Compton managers, these new recruits readily acknowledge that the Compton Way requires personal approaches to ask for a gift – but rarely do they see the need to put as much thought into applying that same principle to enlisting the team.

An experienced chairman will regularly be rethinking and reinventing devices to recruit new visitors throughout the campaign. A useful way to approach this challenge is to imagine you are being approached to join this team, and consider how you would react when asked. As a guide, consider, 'Is this the most personal way I could be approached and do I know what exactly is being asked of me if I joined this team?'

The ultimate test of leadership by example comes when there is a realisation that while you as chairman are doing your utmost to win this campaign, you have the courage to allow others to take over and own the success that will doubtless follow. Team building is the cornerstone of any winning campaign.

### When the going gets tough ...

Leadership has a powerful effect on the progress of a campaign, particularly when things do not go according to plan. We've seen some exceptional volunteer chairmen apply one or all of the following pointers when successfully implementing the Compton Way.

*Decide to win*

Fundraising is usually not at the top of the list of 'must dos' for most people. It is a task they undertake because of what success will bring about. Yet, often other more immediate demands for you, your team and your organisation can take precedence, if you let them. As campaign chairman begin by deciding to win this campaign by a particular time and articulate this priority through your campaign plan, so everyone who joins the fundraising team can make a clear decision to join you and make it happen.

*Focus on asking*

What happens between meetings is what counts. A wise fundraising chairman once said that, 'All I want to know is who asked who for a gift, for how much and when we can expect an answer.'

So much fundraising management activity can in fact mask what is really important in a capital campaign. When your campaign total fails to move up as quickly as required, take a moment to review how much asking is actually taking place. Consider the list of hot prospects who are presently being asked to give, or will be shortly. By addressing these outcomes, even if the approaches are not successful, progress is being made and your attention can move on to others who in fact may make the gifts you need to win.

In many campaigns we've seen major prospects not approached because they might just say 'no' and the fundraising team would rather live in hope than face the risk of rejection. Although not often acknowledged, this procrastination can kill campaign momentum. As chairman, by acting decisively and focusing on the asking that can be done now, you'll reinvigorate your fundraising team.

*Creating small steps*

When faced with a massive climb ahead, it can be understandably daunting, not just for you but also for the whole fundraising team.

With the help of your campaign manager, consider breaking down the overall task into bite size pieces that can then be dealt with one at a time. In fact, it may be possible to ask parts of your fundraising team to take on a specific goal that in itself is not too off-putting.

This will also enable you as chairman to celebrate successes as the campaign proceeds and in turn build momentum towards eventually reaching the target. Such an approach can prove a highly effective way of working with key members of the team and through this acknowledgement, encourage renewed efforts.

## Professional campaign management

Strong leadership, partnered with professional campaign management has a powerful ability to engage busy and influential volunteers as givers and askers for a capital fundraising campaign.

Accomplished professional campaign managers are rare creatures. Above all else, they need to be good communicators. The experienced campaign manager collects and shares stories that can be used to give credence to the principles of fundraising or to explain in an entertaining way to a visitor, how best to undertake an ask.

The professional has mastered the art of making possible that which would otherwise appear daunting, and can use the tools of this art with great effect. Once the campaign manager has established credibility with the volunteer team he ensures that visitors know what is expected of them and have a simple message they can present in a straightforward way.

Inexperienced campaign managers can fail to realise that their team members are intelligent people who easily recognise *happy talk* when it is bandied around. Busy visitors can readily distinguish sales hype from a clear call to action. What they will listen to and act upon, is straight speaking guidance from someone who has done it before, someone they see as being a solid partner, who will work with them through the ups and downs to reach the target.

## Effective campaign management 'makes things happen' …

In our experience working with a wide variety of clients on vastly different campaigns, when it comes to applying the Compton Way, we have identified some key areas for the professional campaign manager to address, if they are to be effective:

### Urgency

Find a cogent answer to the question, 'Why do we need to do this now?'

A genuine sense of urgency needs to be built into every aspect of your campaign from the very beginning. Campaign managers must keep everyone focused on the limited time available to do the job. Reports need to be frequent, concise and timely, composed of relevant statistics. The chairman and visitors should know from week to week just how many approaches have been made, how many are still to be made and most importantly, exactly what they need to do next. By creating a driving momentum for reaching the target, rather than *nagging* the fundraising team, campaign managers will have taken the first steps to success.

### Empowerment

Campaign managers (even the very best) do not have a magic wand they can wave over a campaign and just make things happen. (This fact has come as a real surprise to some we've encountered.) The finest campaign manager simply cannot achieve the target alone, and they know it. They also know that they cannot say to people 'just do it' and expect to step back and watch it happen.

Successful campaign managers 'build' teams. They foster volunteer leadership, promote team member achievements often attributing their own work to others. Ultimately, through the development of clearly defined areas of responsibility their teams begin to function without the constant reinforcement of the campaign manager. In the end, the sum of the efforts of the many greatly exceeds the performance of one committed manager, with everyone sharing in the success that follows.

## Vision

Every member of the fundraising team needs to understand the vision for the campaign. They need to overcome a fascination with how the money will be raised and become committed to how it will be used. Their personal enthusiasm for the vision is essential, so fuel that interest, build a commitment, and demonstrate that only *they* have the power to make it all happen. In short, sell the dream not the campaign.

## Communication

A strong and varied communications programme is at the heart of a winning capital campaign. Directly and indirectly the vision is presented, reinforced and represented, so that there can be no doubt about what is being proposed, what is needed to make it happen and how important it is. A successful communication process starts even before the campaign manager arrives, with the conduct of the resources study, and develops quickly as a sense of excitement is engendered.

## Remove barriers

As campaign managers, we recognise that there are times when we have to operate outside normal organisational constraints. We focus on outcomes, and to implement the change necessary to win our campaigns, we often have to work around the 'blockers' in the organisation. Being an outside consultant helps, provided we remember to use that objective strength judiciously.

## Winning moments

Premature celebration can make people step back. Success should be responded to by carefully refocusing effort on the next goal to achieve. If handled effectively, success can ignite a campaign and drive it forward by increasing the momentum for achieving the target. If handled ineptly, it can cause the team to become complacent and ready to allow a few to do all the work. Good campaign managers are aware that they must use moments of success with as much care and skill as points of failure in the capital campaign.

### Selecting a campaign manager

When selecting your campaign manager, look for someone who will be a good partner – who will listen, but who is also not afraid of speaking his or her mind. At Compton International, we place a heavy emphasis on the 'attitude' of the prospective campaign manager. Not just whether or not they seem willing. We look to see if they themselves have been volunteer leaders of a not-for-profit organisation. We are interested in what first-hand understanding they have had in being a volunteer leader, through their successes and frustrations.

We also talk with each candidate about their personal giving history and in particular the reasons behind the gifts that they have made. The Compton campaign manager must understand, not in a theoretical sense but in a personal way, just what his or her volunteer leader has undertaken to do and how best to work with them. Our professional development team can then give each Compton manager all the technical training and mentoring they need to do the job, but without this personal appreciation of the volunteer's powerful role, the campaign manager will always be just an administrator rather than an effective partner.

Attitude is also evidenced through the candidate's willingness to become professionally certified, particularly to an international standard such as the CFRE (Certified Fund Raising Executive). This is an intellectually challenging process; as campaign managers they will need to be up-to-date with the latest fundraising practices and know exactly how to handle ethical and regulatory issues. The CFRE requires fundraising professionals to recertify every three years and therefore keep abreast of often fast-moving developments in the sector.

Finally, we look for personal qualities that demonstrate character. Good campaign managers don't necessarily need to have won the VC, but they do need to be able to keep going when everyone around them appears to have lost faith; to find the one way to make things happen, when others gleefully identify the million reasons why it just won't work. In their life history, look for a campaign manager who is 'emotionally tough', not insensitive, but rather can demonstrate that they have managed to keep going through personal adversity to see a project through. Capital campaigning is not for the faint-hearted and you'll need a manager who can help give your campaign the direction it needs through the good and the bad times that inevitably will come.

## 'Nothing astonishes men so much as common sense and plain dealing'

In coining this phase, Ralph Waldo Emerson has encapsulated the essence of what it takes to step beyond the routine and do something astonishing. And let's face it; to win a major capital fundraising campaign requires people to do something 'astonishing'. The genius lies in Emerson's recognition that complexity does not in itself equate to expertise.

In this book, we have endeavoured to 'astonish' you with our 'common sense and plain dealing'. We hope that we have:

- revealed the 'truth' behind why we fundraise the way we do
- rekindled the arts of our profession that we see being lost to those who would prefer to complicate or disguise.

We are the first to acknowledge that we have told you nothing new – no novel scheme or shiny fundraising gimmick – no 'tricks' to help you raise millions the fast way, and no easy transplanting of fundraising models imported from abroad.

The Compton Way is entirely about organised common sense. It is entirely constructed on fundraising principles and practices that have been tried, tested and proven to work for a wide variety of different not-for-profit organisations here in the UK. Why not see what it can do for you?

**'If there is something you own that you can't give away, you don't own it, it owns you.'**

*Albert Schweitzer*

## Summary

- Capital fundraising is not a science, but an art.
- Successful campaigns have two key ingredients: leadership by example and professional campaign management.
- When the going gets tough, campaign leaders need to decide to win; focus on asking; and create small steps towards achieving the target.
- Effective campaign management 'makes things happen' by:
  - creating a genuine sense of urgency
  - empowering their volunteer leadership
  - focusing on the vision for the campaign
  - communicating vigorously
  - finding a way to work around barriers within the organisation to ensure the campaign runs to time and achieves the target
  - using winning moments to motivate the team and build momentum for the campaign.
- When selecting a campaign manager, look for someone who has the right attitude and who will be a good partner.

# Glossary

Awareness programme — The use of communications tools to increase the awareness of a charity, inform a broad public about its work and pave the way for prospective volunteers to express interest in knowing more about a project or programme.

CAF — Charities Aid Foundation

Campaign manager — A professional person who is engaged to direct the day-to-day management of a capital fundraising campaign.

Campaign plan — A document that details how the campaign will be conducted, written to help recruit members of the fundraising team and focus the efforts of the not-for-profit organisation.

Capital fundraising campaign — The process of getting as much money as quickly as possible from, initially, as few prospects as possible, using volunteer-led, peer-to-peer personal approaches for a specific project or programme.

Case for support — A more fully argued version of the case statement.

Case statement — A concise two-page document that tells all that needs to be told; answers all the important questions; reviews the arguments for support; explains the proposed plan for raising the money and shows how gifts may be made.

| | |
|---|---|
| Charity | An organisation that is registered (or exempted) by the Government and serves a charitable purpose. |
| Constituent | A person, group, or other entity with an interest in the not-for-profit organisation's mission; may include clients, staff, volunteers, and donors. |
| CSR | Corporate Social Responsibility |
| Cultivation programme | The process of gaining the interest and involvement of targeted prospective donors and volunteer askers before asking them for high-level gifts and support. |
| Designated gift | Recognition given to a donor for a gift made to a specific project or programme (also known as a restricted gift). |
| DoH | Department of Health |
| Donor | Any person or entity (such as grant-making body, corporation or Government agency), that provides a gift to a not-for-profit organisation (also known as a giver). |
| Gift | The voluntary transfer from a donor of money, intellectual property, or real property to a not-for-profit organisation (also known as a donation). |
| HNW | High Net Worth |
| Legacy | A gift made by a donor as part of their will (also known as a bequest or a planned gift). Can be related to a donor's previous giving to a not-for-profit organisation. |

| | |
|---|---|
| Not-for-profit | An organisation that applies surplus funds to its mission, and cannot distribute its profits to members. Sometimes referred to as a non-profit organisation. |
| PFI | Private Finance Initiative |
| Philanthropy | The desire to promote the welfare of others, expressed especially by the generous donation of money to good causes. |
| Pledge | A documented commitment by a donor to make a gift. |
| Potential | The size of gift that a qualified prospect could make to a capital campaign (as determined by prospect rating). |
| PPP | Public Private Partnership |
| Prospect | Any person or entity (such as grant-making body, corporation or Government agency) that a visitor has access to ask personally for a gift. Prospects may include those who have given previously. |
| Rating | Reviewing prospects to determine what size gift each one could make to a campaign, if asked by the right person, at the right time, in the right place for the right part of the project. |
| Resources study | A qualitative research process that identifies an organisation's readiness to mount a capital campaign by testing the sources of contributable funds and the volunteer workers who will become the champions to give and get them. |

| | |
|---|---|
| Scale of giving | A table demonstrating a pattern of gifts that if secured, would ensure a fundraising goal is achieved. |
| Screening | Sorting prospects from suspects, by scoring each according to their capacity to make a gift; propensity to make a gift; interest in the case and personal access. |
| Suspect | Any person or entity (such as grant-making body, corporation or Government agency) who might have a reason to be interested in a fundraising case and to whom access needs to be forged, to become a prospect. |
| Third Sector | Industry term for the UK not-for-profit sector |
| Tithe | A type of giving based on a percentage of the donor's income. Often used in religious giving where the typical tithe is 10% of the donor's income. |
| Visitor | A volunteer who undertakes peer-to-peer asking of qualified prospects to join them and also make a gift to a not-for-profit organisation. |
| Volunteer | A person who contributes time to serve a not-for-profit organisation as a board member, or as a committee member, in programme delivery, in fundraising, or with other unpaid assistance. |

# Bibliography

Alden and Mowbray Ltd. 1973.
*Fundraising by Charities,*
London: Bedford Square Press.
ISBN: 0-7199-0870-1

Andreasen, Alan R. and Philip Kotler. 1995.
*Strategic Marketing for Nonprofit Organizations,*
New Jersey: Prentice Hall.
ISBN: 0-131-22792-0

Bikson, Nancy and David Wickert. 1999.
*Fundraising from America,*
Lingfield UK: Chapel & York Ltd.
ISBN: 1-9032-9303-0

Bird, Drayton. 1993.
*Commonsense Direct Marketing,*
London: Kogan Page.
ISBN: 0-7494-0996-7

Black, Sam. 1995.
*The Practice of Public Relations* (4th edition),
Oxford: Butterworth Heinemann.
ISBN: 0-7506-2318-7

Bramson, Robert M. 1981.
*Coping with Difficult People,*
New York: The Business Library.
ISBN: 1-8635-0118-5

Burnett, Ken. 1996.
*Friends for Life – Relationship Fundraising in Practice,*
London: The White Lion Press.
ISBN: 0-9518-9712-8

Burnett, Ken. 2002.
*Relationship Fundraising: A Donor Based Approach to the Business of Raising Money,*
London: The White Lion Press.
ISBN: 0-951-89710-1

CAF. 2000.
*Dimensions of the Voluntary Sector,*
London: Charities Aid Foundation.

CAF Annual Report 2004.
*Charity Trends* (25th edition),
London: Charities Aid Foundation.
ISBN: 1-9049-6490-7

Carlson, Mim. 2002.
*Winning Grants Step by Step,*
San Francisco: Jossey Bass Wiley.
ISBN: 0-7879-5876-X

Charity Commission. 2003–04.
*Shaping the Future,*
London: The Stationery Office.
ISBN: 0-10-292878-9

Ciconte, Barbara L. and Jeanne G. Jacob. 2001.
*Fundraising Basics: A Complete Guide* (2nd edition),
Maryland: Aspen Publishers Inc.
ISBN: 0-8342-1890-9

Clarke, Sam and Michael Norton. 1997.
*The Complete Fundraising Handbook* (3rd edition),
London: Directory of Social Change.
ISBN: 1-9003-6009-8

Compton, Everald. 1979.
*Where Have the Christian Stewards Gone?*
Devon: Arthur A. Stockwell.
ISBN: 0-7223-1282-2

Compton, Everald. 1983.
*Living with Money,*
New Zealand: Hodder/Genesis.
ISBN: 0-3403-4299-4

Compton, Everald. 1995.
*The Generosity of Profit; The Creation of Corporate Profits through Community Partnerships,*
Brisbane: Boolarang Press.
ISBN: 0-8643-9188-9

Connors, Tracy Daniel. 2001.
*The Nonprofit Handbook: Management* (3rd edition),
New York: John Wiley & Sons.
ISBN: 0-4713-9799-7

Cumerford, William R. 1978.
*Fundraising: A Professional Guide,*
Ferguson E. Peters Company.
ISBN: 0-9182-1402-5

Cumerford, William R. 1993.
*Start-to-finish Fundraising,*
Chicago: Precept Press.
ISBN: 0-9444-9633-4

Cuthbert, David L. 1992.
*Money that Matters,*
Pretoria: J P van der Walt.
ISBN: 0-7993-1855-8

Dove, Kent E. 2000.
*Conducting a Successful Capital Campaign* (2nd edition),
New York: Jossey Bass Wiley.
ISBN: 0-7879-4989-2

Dove, Kent E. 2001.
*Conducting a Successful Fundraising Program,*
San Francisco: Jossey Bass Wiley.
ISBN: 0-7879-5352-0

Dove, Kent E., Lindauer, Jeffery A., and Carolyn P. Madvig. 2001.
*Conducting a Successful Annual Giving Program,*
San Francisco: Jossey Bass Wiley.
ISBN: 0-7879-5649-X

Dove, Kent E., Lindauer, Jeffery A., and Carolyn P. Madvig. 2002.
*Conducting a Successful Major Gifts and Planned Giving Program,*
San Francisco: Jossey Bass Wiley.
ISBN: 0-7879-5707-0

Fredricks, Laura. 1997.
*Developing Major Gifts: Turning Small Donors into Big Contributors,*
Maryland: Aspen Publishers Inc.
ISBN: 0-8342-1829-1

Grace, Kay, Sprinkel. 1997.
*Beyond Fund Raising: New Strategies for Nonprofit Innovation and Investment,*
New York: John Wiley & Sons.
ISBN: 0-4711-6232-9

Greenfield, James M. 2001.
*The Nonprofit Handbook: Fundraising* (3rd edition),
New York: John Wiley & Sons.
ISBN: 0-4714-0304-0

Greenfield, James M. 2002.
*Fundraising Fundamentals,*
New York: John Wiley & Sons.
ISBN: 0-4712-0987-2

Harrison, Allen F. 1982.
*The Art of Thinking,*
New York: The Business Library.
ISBN: 1-8635-0121-5

Hogan, Cecilia. 2003.
*Prospect Research: A Primer for Growing Nonprofits,*
Sudbury MA: Jones & Bartlett Publishers International.
ISBN: 0-7637-2580-3

Howe, Fisher. 1998.
*Fundraising & the Non-profit Board Member,*
Australia: Governance & Management Pty Ltd and NCNB.
ISBN: 1-8765-5002-3

Hurd, Howard. 1995.
*A Guide to the National Lottery,*
London: Directory of Social Change.
ISBN: 1-8738-6067-6

Institute of Fundraising. 2005.
*Codes of Fundraising Practice,*
London: Institute of Fundraising.

Jordan, Ronald K. and Katelyn L. Quynn. 1994.
*Planned Giving: Management, Marketing and Law* (3rd edition),
New Jersey: John Wiley & Sons.
ISBN: 0-4714-4950-4

Kihlstedt, Andrea. 1997.
*Capital Campaigns: Strategies that Work* (2nd edition),
Maryland: Aspen Publishers Inc.
ISBN: 0-8342-1902-6

Kuniholm, Roland. 1995.
*The Complete Book of Model Fundraising Letters,*
New Jersey: Prentice Hall.
ISBN: 0-1333-4202-6

Lautman, Kay Partney. 2001.
*Direct Marketing for Nonprofits,*
Maryland: Aspen Publishers Inc.
ISBN: 0-8342-1959-X

Levy, Barbara R. and Barbara H. Marion. 1997.
*Successful Special Events: Planning, Hosting and Evaluating,*
Maryland: Aspen Publishers Inc.
ISBN: 0-8342-0935-7

Mixer, Joseph R. 1993.
*Principles of Professional Fundraising: Useful Foundations for Successful Practice,*
San Francisco: Jossey Bass Wiley.
ISBN: 1-5554-2590-9

Nash, T. 2001.
*Sustainable Development – Improving Competitiveness Through Corporate Social Responsibility.*
London: Kogan Page.
ISBN: 1-9015-8060-1

Nash, T. 2002.
*Managing your Software Assets — How to Implement a Proper Software Strategy and Avoid Legal Risks and Exposure,*
London: Kogan Page.
ISBN: 1-9015-8082-2

Nichols, Judith. 2001.
*Pinpointing Affluence in the 21st Century,*
Chicago: Bonus Books.
ISBN: 1-5662-5165-6

Popenoe, Norton and Maley. 1994.
*Shaping the Social Virtues,*
The Centre for Independent Studies Limited.
ISBN: 1-8643-2001-X

Rich, Patricia and Dana Hines. 2002.
*Membership Development: An Action Plan for Results,*
Aspen Publishers Inc.
ISBN: 0-8342-1971-9

Rosso, Henry A. and Eugene R. Tempel. 2003.
*Achieving Excellence in Fundraising (2nd edition),*
San Francisco: Jossey Bass Wiley.
ISBN: 0-7879-6256-2

Seiler, Timothy L. 2001.
*Developing your Case for Support,*
San Francisco: Jossey Bass Wiley,
ISBN: 0-7879-5245-1

Seymour, Harold J. 1992.
*Designs for Fund-Raising — Principles, Patterns, Techniques,*
The Taft Group.
ISBN: 0-9308-0720-0

Warwick, Mal. 2001.
*How to Write Successful Fundraising Letters,*
San Francisco: Jossey Bass Wiley.
ISBN: 0-7879-5652-X

Weinstein, Stanley. 1999.
*The Complete Guide to Fundraising Management,*
John Wiley & Sons.
ISBN: 0-4712-0019-0

Wilberforce, Sebastian. 2001.
*Legacy Fundraising,*
London: Directory of Social Change/Charities Aid Foundation.
ISBN: 1-9003-6093-4

Williams, Karla A. 1997.
*Donor Focused Strategies for Annual Giving,*
Maryland: Aspen Publishers Inc.
ISBN: 0-8342-0896-2

# Index

## C

**Notes:**

**Notes:**

**Notes:**

**Notes:**